Wildflower

The Unfolding Evolution of a Woman

By De Layna Starr Brady

In Loving Memory of

My Grandmothers, Mosella Dixon-Brady & Heleema Ahmad

Beloved Brother and friend, Steven Parmenter

Dedication to: My Mother in Christ, Norma J. Parmenter

Acknowledgements

Brothers and sisters, family and friends alike, although theology backs me up I am being as practical and straight up as I possibly can. In my approach to better reach you, in a place you may not have ever been penetrated spiritually, mentally and/or emotionally. It is important to understand that our testimonies are proof of God's mercy in our lives, and often if not always exposes others.

There is a part of me that sincerely apologizes to those that might be offended.

The other part sincerely advises those who might be offended to get real and **be liberated.** There are too many souls (yours and mines included) to stand by idly and proud, doing nothing for the sake of shame and secrets. The truth will set us free....all of us.

That being said, I like to thank God foremost for guiding my pen and my heart.

The pastors who personally affected my life and spiritual growth, Pastors Calvin and Alice Simpson. The late Bishop Vincent and Mariah Claxton and Bishop Edward L. Branch. Those who inspired me from afar and through television, Joyce Meyers, Paula White, T.D. Jakes, Jamaal Bryant, the late Reverend Gilbert and Andrew Wommack. To my Mothers and big Sisters in Christ and becoming a part of a real family, Norma & Steven Parmenter, Margaret & Colleen McKinney, Nancy Hall, Paulette and La Shawn Brady.

Sam Ella Grasty, Suzette Sharper, Nancy Brady, Ethel Jean Hubbard, Helen Rollins, Doris Morris.

Alice Simpson. Thank you for the love and support, you'll never know how much your motherly and sisterly love has nurtured and helped me in my growth. A very special artist, whom I feel it was divine intervention to stumble across her work, Ashley Coll. Your work has given more vision to mines, thank you.

To my children, Elicia, Erric and Eboni Hall for giving me strength to push forward and press on. If not for you I probably would have given up a long time ago. For letting me know you recognize that strength in me. Let it be an example in your own lives. A few people I still consider friends even though I haven't talked to in years. Donna Monk, Stephenel Mitchell-Mallory, Dana Lowery-Williams and Lynell Marks. I love you guys, you're the roses in my fresh bouquet. My dear friend Renay Lovelady,You're a gem that's real and pure in heart! Terri Giordano and Nina Harrison, My sisters in Philly, you all have been a life line!

The graphic events and profanity in this book may not be acceptable from a religious view point, but with all due respect.... I have to tell it like it is. Need I remind you God knew the incidents before I did. He used me to write them.

(Although this book is mostly fictional in it's story telling

 aspect, it is also derived from real life experiences to

an

extent.)

If he meant for them all to be pretty, he would have left out the ugly. If I have to quote my "characters", I need to be precisely correct about it.

Preface

This is the story of a woman who has known both what it is like to be lusted by a man AND loved by one. Many of us do not know the difference between these two emotions. Many of us settle for one, when the other doesn't seem possible. It shows how due to where we are in our lives emotionally, mentally and spiritually, what we will allow and submit to. How we can become disillusioned and enslaved to the deceptive images of love. We have been keeping ourselves down with our very own perceptions of self, in a weak period in time.

No one can subject us to anything we aren't willing to accept. Are you accepting negative behavior in your life from men for their affections? Did you invite it into your homes and beds after it was already evident in your first encounter that he was abusive and a womanizer? If you have answered yes to either question, please read this book with an open mind and heart. A strong desire for more out of life and love. When we accept less for ourselves, we dishonor ourselves and God. God intended for every woman to feel like a Queen and act like a lady. Unfortunately, we're not always groomed with such etiquette are we? Circumstances have stolen our identities, our innocence and our self esteem. What do we do when we feel this hopeless? We seek God and find our true selves.

A lady is like a flower, a wildflower. The first time I heard the O'Jays sing this beautiful ballad called

Wildflower, there was an edification. If you've ever heard this song, you understood that the writers have compassion for this woman. That they both empathize with and respect her for her strength and frailty. My character, Delilah Bristroe is a lady coming into her own. She's one of the unfortunate sisters who has weathered many storms early on. Yet she has so much grace and strength in her stride, that you can't help but to draw from her spirit. When she fails, she takes responsibility without being too hard on herself for too long. She knows if she spends too much time dwelling on her mistakes, she'll never rise to meet new challenges. Mistakes are necessary experiences for success. There was a time when Delilah believed that her failures and mistakes defined her and her whole life. She became hopeless and passive. She would soon understand the root of all her confusion. Why her soft petals took so long to unfold and blossom into a free and gentle flower, growing wild.

Prelude: To a True love

Sometimes the strongest of us can fall prey to the deception of a commitment- phobic brother(brother of any race).

The ones who can get the "cookies" without leaving his prints or claims on the "jar", but never fail to leave on your hearts a scar. The ones who know how to maneuver   and   manipulate   around   your standards(which aren't firmly placed to begin with), and self worth in order to get "full service at discount prices". You can't really blame anyone for trying to negotiate a bargain can you? No, but you have to remember YOU are not an object.

When it comes to your self worth, there is no bargaining. You can't say, "I'm not easy" and have sex on the first night just because he wants to. Desire and approval are two different things. He may want it but he doesn't approve, don't get it twisted. You can't pay for the first date and dinner when he asked YOU out, because you'll never see a future dinner unless you're paying for it or cooking it for him.

You see, we set the stage for how things come into play for us. Often times, brothers see us as worthy prospects and are eager to please. After several attempts to woo us and win us over with extravagant gestures and gifts, that each left them dumbfounded as to why we don't see ourselves the way they do...it ends. If they decide to stick around, you can almost always bet it won't be the same. He thought the world of you therefore, tried to give you the world. Each time, you declined with remarks like, 1. "Oh that's too expensive" and he's thinking, "Oh so you're saying you're not worth it? That this THING is worth more than you are?!"

2. You: "Oh, but I didn't get you anything." He's thinking," I didn't expect
you to either, jeez!"

3. You: "Oh, I don't need anything I'm straight." He's thinking, "Well I guess you're saying you don't need or want me either. I guess I can't do nothing for you, so I'll find someone who lets me be the man I am."

Honey trust me when I tell you this, your words will come back to haunt you.

If you get one of these brothers, you'll have plenty of time to be modest later. Now you're wondering why he doesn't do anything but take from you.

Never asks you out, never buys you anything and it's just a matter of time before he's gone. Think back, I bet it was you who set yourself up. Either that, or this brother was never even trying and that's your fault too.

We have to stop taking ourselves OFF, the pedestal God put us on and a good man can see us on. Generally, people will treat you the way you treat yourself.

Once he decides you would rather be his whore than his queen, he won't change his mind again. If the Lord God Almighty finds you worthy and lovable enough to dwell in you, so can man dwell with you. God has placed so much value on you as a person, and is in fact trying to command his presence in your life to bring to you what you deserve.... the very best and nothing less.

Stop blocking your blessings, let "Ruth and Boaz" come forth in unity.

Chapter One

On a cool November day, leaves scattered about the streets in a beautiful mass of russet color. Things were finally settling down in this hype inner- city neighborhood. Particularly Burrough Street, where all the action was usually happening. Whether it was some young thugs getting arrested, some gangster or pimp slapping a simple young girl around. Thugs getting shot, thugs shooting craps, silly young girls standing on top of cars dancing or the favorite dysfunctional family next door that kept you thoroughly entertained airing their dirty laundry outside. The things that happened outside on Burrough Street, made you fear what you couldn't see on the inside behind closed doors. The area was so close to the suburbs and looked so much like the suburbs, that if you were just passing through at a good time (like today), you'd think you were amongst the most civil, refined socialites the city had to offer.

The day was looking good, although the skies were gray with a few bees lost in translation that summer had come and gone. Delilah stood in front of her two

-story Colonial style house swinging her rake frantically at the bees. Clearly , she was

in a funk and even the bees weren't feeling her and headed south. This was a rare breed too, they weren't that easy to get rid of. They were bolder than rats. Earlier that summer, Delilah watched these killer bees attack a nest of baby birds and ate them to the bones like a chicken dinner. They later frightened the cat that hung out in her yard out of a can of tuna she had left.

Delilah didn't know what kept her in the house more, the bees or the thugs.

All she did know was she didn't want neither to catch up with her. Her mood today could have been for a number of reasons, maybe she wasn't down for the clean up everyone else was so cheerfully doing. She just felt obliged to, not being the most domestic person. You couldn't tell from the looks of her, but she participated by keeping her property decent. She didn't have a garden and beds of flowers, but hey the grass was green thanks to enough rain.

She was the last to come out and join in with leaves piled up to her door, but you could bet she meant for most of them to be finishing up with theirs when she started with hers. Don't get it "twisted", Delilah was friendly.

It's just that people had a way of taking more of her time than she was willing to share and she'd never get anything done if the conversation was interesting enough.

Since she was a thinker, being in solitude was ideal for her. A lot of time passed if she could sort some things out in her head while she worked.

When she wasn't feeling sociable, she did her best to avoid people not wanting to spread a negative vibe. Though that was being considerate, the needy, dysfunctional family took it personally....every time. Even if she waited for them to go inside, they would come right back out when they saw she was outside. She could be reading the bible and they would still stand on their porch right on the other side of the drive way, and yell her name. When she would finally look up and answer, they'd ask, "What you doing or what you reading?" and she'd think, "It doesn't matter WHAT I'm reading, the point is I AM reading and you can SEE that!"

Maybe she was just pissed at the world right now. After all, she had just called off a two month affair she'd been having with G-Money. He had approached her as Gerard, the ambitious, practical brother full of positive energy, fun and charm. Slowly G-Money(the guy or shall I say thug, the rest of the hood knew him as?), started to surface. Even as a thug, he didn't lose his appeal on her, not right away. In fact, she began to reconsider her bigotry for the Thug mentality. Suddenly, they weren't ALL ignorant and worthless beings who's only reason for living was chasing paper, collecting women and other fine possessions. In which they knew the price of all and value of none. She was pissed because even though she had the good sense to call

it off, it was two months too late. Too late to say no harm was done, too late to save herself.... from herself. It wasn't long before Delilah could see the street name was what this man was about, in and out, to and from.

Ironically enough, for somebody who loved chasing paper, he wasn't catching any.

Still, he was so spiritual and humane. A compassionate

thug? It was like, "Wow!" he listened to her, with a boyish innocence and he was attentive, sensual, strong and gorgeous. He had goals and plans of his own and his head seemed to

always be in the clouds or another sphere. The problem was, he didn't know how to handle present day situations for always planning for future situations.

Gerard didn't have to do too much to win Delilah over either. Another reason she's so pissed. Everything he did scored big points with her and she isn't easily impressed. She didn't play hard to get with this one, then again , he didn't give much reason to. He came in the door right, like he knew it wasn't going to be easy and played his best hand upfront. Therefore, she felt her status as Queen was already recognized. He had simply blind sided her by doing things she didn't expect him to do knowing how to get next to her.

He had upped the ante on his conquest and sped up the time line to conquer.

When he did something for her, he didn't stick around long enough for her to thank him, let alone invite him in. He would come by with flowers or "just because" gifts and say, "I got to run, I'll call you later." She dug that about him big time. So much it put a smile on her face, and that's all he would stay around long enough to see before taking off to chase that paper.

You can bet YOUR paper he knew she was wetting her panties for him too.

Every time he got that smile, he knew he could get that "kitty" too. The chase is much better than the capture, try to remember this ladies. Sometimes it's simply not worth catching unless there's going to be a release too. A man will hold out longer than you can just to salvage the moment to seize. See he must be in control. The longer it takes, the better the chances it will last. Nobody appreciates anything they didn't have to work hard to get like something they did. Here it comes, the blow. She gave in one month after they met. That's not a whole lot of time to get to know someone. A few days after their first sexual encounter, that's when his whole routine changed. She realized it was

organized crime just like everything else in his life.

A good businessman knows how to buy and sell. He knows what you want before he even approaches you because he's got buyers on the look out. Telling him what's hot and what's not, what's quality and what's cheap. Delilah wasn't upset about this, she was impressed. He had done his homework, you see it takes game to recognize game. If you like playing chess, you know what I mean. You know each game is different and unpredictable at it's best. This was the point of that new peak for her, a new high. This was proof that he was not wasting her time for amusement and being thoroughly entertained. It didn't matter that he was leading this show because if you could lead Delilah(the temptress who's easily bored), you were doing the impossible. She even complimented him for his feats and joked with him about some of his tactics. He even laughed with her and was impressed by her wit and sense of humor. Though he had tried to use the "boyish" innocence again, he could see she was no, longer buying it. "That's cool" he said. "There's plenty more where that came from."

THAT was the first cue she blew off. By this time, Delilah was really feeling this brother. She was the type that liked to get close to the flame without getting burned. She loved the dark suspense like she loved a good film Noir.

She saw a lot of potential and had so much in common with him. They were like two peas in a pod, except he was always trying to get out of the pod. He wasn't interested in a relationship, he was trying to sell the "friends with benefits" package to her. She was in love with him, but he was in lust with her.

Now the ride feels like going down a mudslide and landing in quicksand trying to keep from sinking. She suddenly felt dirty and cheap because he wasn't even willing to compromise. You can't go back and change course at this point. You can't reroute your entire strategy. All you can do is try and save face right? You'd be wise to concede, cut your losses and move on at this point. Delilah tried because she was proud and dignified, but she was also arrogant. I mean dude was teasing her to her face that she wasn't going to get him. I mean like hang in there. She didn't like losing and certainly not bad. She had to redeem her reputation and hoped to still win him in the end as a bonus. She was hopelessly devoted like Olivia Newton-John's song. She heard her mind say,

"Fool forget him", but her heart was saying, "Don't let him go, hold on til the end." That's just what she intended to do too cause she was in love you dig?

Now suppose that was the holy spirit saying, "Fool forget him" and that "kitty" saying, "Don't let go, hold on until the end"? How does she determine which is which? Prayer my sisters. If she was still talking to God as much as she was pleading and negotiating with Gerard, she might have noticed the voice of the spirit and that of the flesh. She might have gotten him just because she THOUGHT she wanted him or realize she didn't have to have him sooner.

You know the worst part about of it for her? She did know the difference, which explains the misery she finds herself wallowing in.

We're going to go back in time now, because this isn't the first time this has happened to Delilah..... but it was the last time. You see, there is a method to the madness, a pattern to this type of a behavior. We want to know where it starts in order to find out where and how it ends.

Chapter Two

Delilah Simone Bristroe A.K.A. Lilah, born May 28th, 1966. Father was murdered, lived with Mother and Step Father most of her childhood. A dark child with long , thick black hair and big brown eyes. These were happier times, so that's what they tell her. She doesn't remember, not one Christmas, not one birthday, not one hug from Mommy or Daddy..... nothing. Her first memory of

her childhood was age four, watching the Jackson Five, Fat Albert and Jiminy Cricket cartoons. Mickey Mouse and Jiminy Cricket were on the TV screen in every nightmare Lilah had for years to come while she was being raped by her stepfather's sixteen year old nephew. This horrific ordeal went on everyday

for a week. She remembers kinder-garden, but not the first grade. By the time she was seven, not only had she lost her innocence a few years back, she was losing her identity as well. Her Step dad didn't seem to like her very much and everyday her Mother left to go to work, he would make sure she knew he didn't like her.

He spent hours calling her names, telling her she was ugly and that he wasn't her daddy. He would give her younger sister(his daughter) gifts and treats and tell her not to share with Lilah. Lilah's four year old sister was more mature and could feel this was wrong. She would share things with Lilah when he left the room and sneak things to her if she went to her room. He often did this like it was a ritual, a deed that had to be done for him to be happy with himself.

Lilah was almost certain he was the devil, because his words hurt her more than his whippings. Usually her mother gave the whippings, and usually her mother always sided with him and believed all of his lies regarding Lilah. One day he told Lilah her mother would never throw him out. She'd throw her out first and he'd always come first. You know what? That's probably the first thing he said to that poor little girl that was true. After years of watching him flirt and solicit sex from her mother's nieces and sisters then deny it. Jump on her mother, shoot at her mother she was too bitter and angry to be afraid of him anymore.

By the time she could finally recall a Christmas she was ten. Watching her drug addicted step father fall all over her and her sister's gifts and breaking them.

He even knocked the tree to the floor. Lilah moved out with her mother and sister a few times, but they would always miss him and go back. Not Lilah, she asked her Aunt if she could stay the last time they packed up and went back.

That must have been the first time she felt a sense of peace and security in her life, even though she still felt ugly and unlovable.

Her Aunt was nice to her, she was even affectionate

and showed concerned for Lilah. The cousins were cool too, but as far as having a home, she wanted to belong in her own family. So she went back her last year in Junior High School.

She had grown up too, mostly legs because she was tall for her age. She was a cute black girl who was totally unaware of it. It wasn't easy being a dark-skinned girl in the seventies. No boy could see beyond her complexion, so now on top of being ugly she was too dark. It wouldn't matter if she wasn't ugly anyway because she was dark. Dark seemed to equal an automatic ugly in those days. Since she already had it embedded in her brain that she was ugly, that was no shock to her. Still, she was starting to dig boys now.

Ironically enough, every boy she was attracted to was light-skinned, white/Italian, Spanish or Asian. Usually with green or hazel eyes, straight or curly hair. Isn't that something? The little black girl who's discriminated against for being dark, don't like dark boys. Could it be with a Negro breathing down her neck and spitting foul words in her face endlessly and having been raped by one of his people, she was just disgusted with the Negro man?

Lucky for her, things were taking a turn and changing to her benefit around 1979. She was starting to come out of her protective shell, gaining a little confidence in herself. Pushing back the tomboy for the girl who likes talking on the phone with boys and shop with her girlfriends. She was getting plenty of attention from some of the cutest boys now. Because of her experience with the first male figures in her life, she wasn't about to be dominated by them no matter how much she liked and appreciated the attention. When they tried to go too far,it was over. Somewhere between graduating from middle school and moving to a better neighborhood, her step dad publicly humiliated her.

Grabbed her by the ponytail and dragged her home, now everybody knew she was an abused child! She was so hurt and embarrassed. She got hold of a butcher knife and tried to end his miserable life that day, but her Uncle contained her.

Her friends felt so bad for her and wanted to help, but that wasn't enough to keep Lilah from going back into her shell of shame and despair. He didn't touch again after that though for years. He had his biggest weapon still, he'd used her own Mother to hurt her. I think one of the hardest things for a child is having two parents that aren't parents to them at all.

The new house had the same old family dysfunctions going on it, nothing had changed but their address and having a new addition to the family, her little brother. Step father's misery seemed to grow every year as he graduated from one drug to the next. One affair after another, and all while being dependent on Delilah's mother to provide for him and his lifestyle. The only thing that caused Lilah to come out of her shell again was being in a new neighborhood, with new people who didn't know how messed up her and her family were. She always needed to be able to relate to the outside world, because she felt alienated in her own home. She drew from her imagination and lived there most of the time. Creating stories and fantasies that eased her pain and kept her from feeling alone and rejected.

She could never see or feel the love her sister received, never felt like a real part of the family, unless there were relatives visiting. Most of her relatives seemed to adore her on both sides of the family when she was growing up. That was a comfort and encouragement, if only they never had to leave and go back home. I think they knew she was an outcast before she did.

It wouldn't be two whole years later before Delilah would meet her first love.

She was turning fifteen the day this handsome young man would ask her mother if he could take her for ice cream and to the arcade. Kary was a dream come true. He was her best friend, her boyfriend and a father figure all wrapped into one big, muscular, athletic, tough and compassionate(did I say handsome?) brother. Through the years, this courtship grew stronger, but not without the dysfunctions of the family having it's affect. Her stepfather brought his trifling, evil games into play here too, often tempting Kary to want to whoop his ass. Kary made Lilah proud because he was always the better man and turned the other cheek. More of a man than stepfather would ever be, because he was only Eighteen.

Then of course, there was that time when Lilah's

mother responded to Kary's request to take her Downtown for dinner and a movie. It was a shock to both Lilah and Kary when she replied by saying,"You can take her and throw her in the river for all I care after what she did to you!" "This is your daughter you're suggesting someone mistreats! That said a lot about how you yourself treat her." Lilah thought, and she was willing to bet her life Kary thought so too.

Now Lilah had punished (or should I say retaliated against) Kary two weeks earlier by letting him see her with another boy. This happened because Kary got distracted by a new girl on his block after two years of dating Lilah. Simply because everyone else liked her. She had her eyes On Kary because she knew he wasn't available, and he wanted to impress his friends. He had for the first time, humiliated and hurt Lilah by flirting with this girl. She had given him an ultimatum, your new friend or me and he said he wasn't giving up his new friend so she broke up with him. Lilah started hanging out with Stephen and Kary found out and pleaded with her to take him back. Of course she did.

She just needed to remind him she wasn't going to be ignored every time some other pretty girl came along. That he was going to respect her and their relationship or there wasn't going to be any relations between them.

When they got Downtown that night Kary told Delilah, "You know your mother is jealous of you right?" She answered, "No, why would she be?"

"Because you got somebody that loves you now." Delilah smiled in agreement, but she also felt guilty. Like she really didn't deserve it somehow. If her mother was jealous instead of happy for her, how could she be happy? During her Senior year, Kary joined the army with the intent to build a life for them. They were supposed to get married after she graduated and move to California.

Again, the dysfunctional family interfered. This time it was her sister who contributed to a misunderstanding between she and Kary, because it involved her sister's boyfriend. Kary called the whole thing off with Lilah. It later came to light that the night in question was never worth the cost of her losing the love of her life.

Her knight in shining armor, her Prince. She had lost him for nothing. To this day, she knows it pleases all who envied what she had with him. She saw him again, but he was married with a child and it wasn't even for love. Even though they had agreed things shouldn't have ended over a jealous sister's indiscretion and deception, they had both moved on. The love and admiration was ever fresh between them and that gave her a sense of peace that at least he didn't hate her and believe she was unfaithful that summer many years ago anymore.

Kary was in a marriage of convenience and even though Lilah knew he deserved better , she could see how much he loved his daughter and how happy he was around her. To think it all happened because he didn't believe her, Kary knew better than anyone what Delilah had to suffer at home and why she moved when he left for the Army.

Delilah felt if Kary didn't believe in her anymore, nothing mattered. When they split, she became the promiscuous type. Smoking marijuana and sexing all the pretty boys became a way to cope for her. To avoid the pain she still felt over losing Kary. She didn't seem to care about her reputation, she was hurting and feeling low, she had already been painted to be worthless to Kary. Some times people take comfort anyway they can get it, and at this particular time,she felt she had nothing to gain or lose. Kary was her protector and savior.

The only one she had ever discovered in her life. The knowledge of a savior that would never turn on her hadn't been discovered yet. To her surprise on her nineteenth birthday, her mother showed up. She picked Lilah up from "The Island",a little place across the bridge her and her "pretty boy friends" hung out at and got high. She gave Lilah a diamond and emerald ring set in gold and they just drove around and talked. She told Lilah she should come home and get off the streets. That she was going to ruin herself and that "those people" didn't care about her.

She seemed sincere about helping her daughter, but she could have been more concerned how her daughter's behavior was going to make HER look. I mean so much evidence supports that theory than being truly concerned for Lilah did.

Yet, all poor Lilah could see and hear was that "

Mama wanted her to come home." There had been times when Lilah had runaway and had not been home or called for at least a week, and her Mother showed no concern at all. In fact, the people she would be staying with would end up calling her mother out of concern to find out why she wasn't looking for her daughter. She'd say, "Oh, I was JUST about to make a police report. Is she alright?" Oh please stop! Delilah had dropped out of high school her senior year during the last semester. She was popular, and a honor student with a three point eight grade average. She was so terrified she did everything she could to avoid it. Her Mother missed her elementary graduation, she stood alone but by the grace of God an Aunt happened to be there for her friend's son and stood in for her too.

Middle school graduation, Mother and Grandmother were there. Her mother bought the material her grandmother made her suit with. It seemed special enough and like she was important that day. There was no doubt in her mind her Grandmother loved her AND pitied her.

Subconsciously, Lilah had given up on herself. Her mother didn't seem to believe in her or really care if she made it or not most of the time. It was hard being called to get your diplomas, awards, certificates and honors with no one being there to share your accomplishments with. So Lilah skipped the whole thing and didn't graduate, a decision she would later regret.

Four years later, Delilah was inspired by her younger

sister who had also dropped out and had a baby. When her sister got her general equivalence diploma, their mother went all out. Inviting the whole family to the graduation and dinner afterwards. What was she thinking? Was Lilah that delusional that she

thought her mother would be just as excited for her when she got hers just a year later? She had scored higher on the tests AND finished the course for her certificate in medical office management which her sister dropped

before completing. When she told her mom the date of her graduation, do you know what this woman said?! She said, "It's your graduation, you go!" Well I'll be damned! That's exactly how Delilah felt... damned to all goodness and straight to hell. She didn't go to that graduation because no one would be there. She didn't even mention it to those she knew WOULD come, like her Grandmother and Aunts. At least she had her diploma now and some skills she conceded.

These scars had started growing tumors instead of healing, you feel me? Every time she got up, she was knocked back down and sometimes literally.

Chapter Three

Delilah packed her things up and left the wild life, "The island" and the pretty boys behind. Thinking things were going to actually be different. Since her mother had asked her to come home, what else could it mean? I told you she was delusional, still full of hope or both. Step dad wasn't happy about her return obviously. He thought he had finally gotten rid of "Miss Smart Ass".

He did everything he could to provoke her daily. Trust me, you've never met a pettier punk than this one. I mean a grown man picking on a little girl since like age five or six?! Then "Mom" is like, "Well has he ever touched you sexually?" No but he touched her every other way that's offensive and cruel.

His people had touched her sexually, so yeah in a way he's still responsible.

If he had been a real father and provider to her, none of it would have happened. I'd like to think Delilah could have had a better childhood. Hard as it is to look at her life, I know the bitter simply came before the sweet, because God had a plan all along. Step Dad wanted her out of that house one way or another. He told lies about Lilah being with men, claiming to have witnesses who never came forward.

He didn't even need them because Mama liked to believe the worst about Lilah.

If she wasn't given the worst case scenario, she created one herself. I guess that made it easier for her not to have to love Lilah. That burned Lilah bad, worst than any name you could call her and harm you could inflict on her body.

When that didn't send her running again, he kept provoking her with little silly things around the house. Like going behind her messing up everything she'd cleaned up. When she confronted him about it without being vulgar, he called her a bitch spitting all over her face. She told him she didn't appreciate being called such things and to stop spitting on her. "Bitch, bitch, bitch!", with more spit followed. Like it was so wrong to ask him to stop spilling stuff on purpose for her to wipe up. Since she was bending over backwards to keep the peace?

Delilah attempted to walk away when he hauled off and slapped her. That's when they fought all through the house back and forth, from room to room. When he realized she wasn't backing when she'd had enough, she started punching and kicking back and the brawl went all down, he picked up a chair and broke it over her backside.

Then grabbed a mop and beat her with it until it snapped. Even though she was defeated and in bad shape, all she could think about was what her little brother had witnessed. He had run out of the house and was hiding. She didn't know if he was afraid or felt bad because he couldn't help his sister from being beat by his father. She made her way outside and yelled for him, but he wouldn't come out or answer. Delilah limped next door and asked her neighbor if she could use his phone. Her sister was away that summer and Mother was at work. She told the guy next door what had happened, he was her age and he advised her to call the police instead of her mother.

Delilah did not, feeling her mother would be upset about it. She wanted to believe what he had done to her would be enough for her to see what a monster he was. The first thing this woman said when Lilah informed her she would be calling the police next was, "No! I'll be right home, stay where you are until I get there. Don't call nobody else, I'm coming straight home." Delilah believed her, she trusted a woman who had let her down one hundred times before. The neighbor accommodated Lilah while taking care of his paraplegic mother. It took her mind off her pain and problems for awhile watching him. She thought about

all the summers this same boy had been sleeping under the back porch of this very house she was sitting in. Eating out of a dog dish while his siblings were inside eating at the table.

Now here he was taking care of this evil woman who treated him that way. She was terrified of him too, you could tell by the look in her eyes she was afraid karma had come for her. Delilah almost cried because you could see that although he had the power to hurt her, all he wanted was to love and care for her. None of her other children took care of her now that she was helpless.

Lilah started to think she probably didn't have it half

as bad as this guy did, when she realized three hours had gone by and she still didn't see her mother's car outside. She asked if she could use the phone again and he nodded yes as he fed his mother. Something told her to call her Aunt since her mother had been off work for hours now. "Hello?" "Hi Aunt Sally", Delilah said. This was the Aunt she had lived with for awhile. "Oh Hi Lilah, how are you sweetheart?" "Fine", she lied. Though her aunt's voice was soothing, she was anything but fine.

"Is my mother over there?" she asked. "She sure is, you want to talk to her?" Lilah's eyes bulged out of her head she was so stunned with disbelief."Did you say that she IS there?" Lilah asked again to make sure she heard right.

She didn't expect her instinct to be right even if she followed it. "Yeah, she's sitting right here drinking beer and watching movies."

"How many times can your heart break into a million pieces, and still feel like it's breaking in yet another million each time it's broken again by the same person?! Delilah thought. "Lilah?" Aunt Sally said softly as if she was getting the impression something was wrong. Yes, uh no I don't want to talk to her, bye." Lilah hung up the phone and tears streamed down her face. The guy could tell how everything went and shook his head in disappointment. "She's at my Aunt's, she's not coming. She doesn't care what he did to me! I should have called the police", she said as she gained control of her tears and turned them into anger. "I told you, you should still call them right now", said the guy. She didn't, not knowing if she still didn't want to upset her mother or too upset herself that her mother lied to stall her. She just asked for a dollar . "Thank you, I'll catch the bus to my Grandmother's", she said.

A friend(who was almost her first love, but didn't have time for virgins) picked her up at the bus stop. It was obvious to him she was sad as she gazed out of the window on her side. It felt like the end of the world to her. She watched the pavement roll behind as the car went forward, the way she felt life was rolling over her.

Mack tried everything to get her to smile, but it just wasn't happening.

She thanked him for the ride and said good bye. Mack yelled back,"Hey,is it alright if I come by tomorrow to see how you're doing?" "Yeah sure" she answered attempting to walk up the porch stairs. She told Grandma what happened and where Mama was. Grandma made her a bath with epsom salt, then rubbed her now black and blue bruises down with winter green alcohol.

Her face was swollen, slightly bruised and scratched up. Grandma's so upset, she made Lilah show her Uncle the bruises. He went, "It looks like that nigga needs his ass whooped by a real man!" Her cousin was talking about having him jumped.

Grandma said they shouldn't be talking that way, that two wrongs didn't make a right. She was a very spiritual and religious woman. Delilah went to bed, it had been a long day. Too long and so wrong!

While she was sleeping, Grandma had called Aunt Sally's to talk to her other daughter (Lilah's mother). Who had probably confessed by now, the real reason she had been hanging out at her sister's house like a coward. Grandma wanted to know why she left Lilah hanging like that, because she understood that was the worst part in it all for Lilah. Clearly, she didn't want to have to take a side and all of her excuses were so pathetic that relatives couldn't stand to listen to her anymore and were leaving the room or house. Coming by Grandma's to check on Lilah's condition. Everybody it seemed, except her mother. She had stayed away until there were no more bruises or evidence of the assault.

Grandma begin trying to heal the poor girl's other scars, the internal ones.

Not being on the surface, it was pretty hard to tell how severe they were.

With all the buried trauma this last ordeal brought out, that had been repressed over the years, Grandma felt it wasn't nothing Jesus couldn't fix.

"Delilah, you know you got to forgive him don't you?", Grandma said. "I hate that man, I'll never forgive him! My own Mama loves him more than she loves me." She said without even showing emotions. Grandma just sighed and looked at Delilah with compassion and said, "You're not hurting anybody but yourself with hatred. It will make you sick and keep you down." Her words upset Lilah even more. "How could you expect me to forgive that man?!

How am I supposed to just say it's okay, it don't matter what he did anymore?!" She asked bewildered. "Look at the power he has over your life because you WON'T forgive him. Be free Lilah, be free" Grandma said while rubbing Lilah's hand. She didn't want to upset her anymore so she returned to her sewing machine. Lilah rose from the table and walked away mumbling, "Aint no way, aint no way." After going to bed and being asleep a few hours, she couldn't sleep anymore for a rumbling in her belly. She had been rehashing events in her sleep, trying to give herself justification not to forgive. She rose up on her knees in the center of the bed, with both arms wrapped around and pressed against her belly. Pressing her arms closer and rocking, she cried freely as she released those memories. Like projector cards playing and ejecting from her memory's files. She could feel the weight on her heart growing lighter and lighter as if there had been a heavy load there affecting her breathing. The sickening, nauseous feeling that had woke her was easing up. Her stomach settled down and tears welled up. " I forgive him Lord, I forgive him. Oh God, please forgive me!" Delilah wailed.

She must have cried into the early dawn and it would've been almost impossible for Grandma and Uncle Jordan not to hear her. Nobody came in that room, maybe they understood what was happening. It was definitely a good thing, the holy spirit had come upon her and helped her dispose of her bondage.

At least the part regarding her step dad , in which she would later understand he was only part of the real reason for her pain, and not the core of it.

Grandma must have done some serious praying on her behalf because she didn't know how. She knew she was better for it. When she told her grandmother about the experience she looked relieved but not surprised. You get the feeling she was on the other side of that door experiencing it right with Lilah. Lilah didn't even need coercion to find the Lord now, something her Grandmother was known for. To church she went.

Chapter Four

Things look so much brighter now. Life is good! Delilah is healthy, happy and holy.

After two years of putting her life back together with the help of her spiritual mother and father, life had taken a positive turn. Her Pastor who bought her a bible, helped her find a job and taught to have faith and hope again. It had been a long time. Pastor Kilborn was like the father she never had, probably better.

He was easy going, you could talk to him about anything. Things you probably only felt comfortable talking to the same sex about. Natalie, a middle aged white woman, who attending the church on week nights was drawn to Delilah instantly.

She thought Delilah was so cute and bright. She decided to be her mentor.

She took Delilah in shortly after getting to know her, it seemed they needed each other. Natalie had been estranged from her youngest daughter against her will, the way Lilah had been with her mother. They both had hope for reconciliations, but for now they had each other. Natalie is a good woman, she's all heart. The things she'd do to try to give a glimpse of what a mother's love and bonding felt like. She'd lay Lilah's head in her lap and brush her hair. Hold her in her arms and stroke her backside with soft caressing hands. Make her warm milk before tucking

her in and kissing her good night. Delilah was twenty

years old by then, but something new and extraordinary was happening to make her feel like a ten year old. She was living in the suburbs where few blacks lived but more worked.

She was going to church and hanging out with her rich white friends, male and females. Learning to manage her money and responsibility. Everything seemed normal and she fit in just fine without having to be untrue to herself.

She hadn't taken anyone seriously even though she'd been out with a few guys.

They were all platonic rather than romantic. Every Wednesday, she and Natalie went to Pastor Kilborn's church still. One Wednesday, Natalie spotted a new guy.

She was very aware and observant, nothing got by her. According to Natalie, he was very handsome and she was trying to fix Lilah up with him. She could be over bearing and controlling in such a gentle way. You wouldn't even realize she was bossing you sometimes. She's very soft spoken and good intentioned, that really you wouldn't remember what your arguments were against something she suggested. She gives so much of herself, that it was hard or down right unacceptable to not want to please her. Not only was Lilah in agreement on how handsome he was when she finally saw him, but she already knew who he was.

He had lived around the corner from Aunt Sally. She had never played with him or his sister, because they were a couple of pompous jerks. They were bi-racial and wouldn't play with dark skinned kids, even though their mother was dark.

Lilah scoffed at the recall of his attitude back then.

This made Natalie even happier ,she didn't have to make an introduction. She would not have hesitated to do so, rather asked to or not. Lilah approached him after service and asked if he remembered her. He politely said he did not.

However, he DID know who she was from his friends that went to church there.

Telling him how "straight and unmoved" she was from her path and couldn't be tempted. That she was fine and nobody had gotten with her because she was "down with the Lord." He didn't tell her that though, that was HIS little secret. He did know her cousin, Aunt Sally's son directly. They started reminiscing about some mutual friends they had then, without ever having contact with each other and of course they both knew why that was. She was still dark-skinned, was he still a pompous jerk?! It didn't matter because Lilah wasn't interested. She was just being friendly to a familiar face. That wouldn't stop Natalie from inviting him over for dinner and suggesting he and Lilah study the bible together sometimes. Kyle seemed very honest and sincere. He was charming, but he never went overboard with compliments to try to impress Delilah. He talked about his girlfriend who lived on a college campus a lot.

He and Lilah were just friends hanging out and she

was cool with that. One night they were at church and Kyle's friend offered to give Lilah a ride home if she wanted to stay late. So Natalie left Lilah with friends her own age.

On the way home, she and Kyle were riding in the back seat and he confided in her that he really liked her. That he wanted to be with her instead of his girlfriend. "But you ARE with your girlfriend, I can't believe you are that impulsive", Lilah snapped unimpressed. "What do you mean? I hardly ever see her. Like Pastor Kilborn said, it's hard to date someone who isn't saved anyway", he said in his defense. Kyle leaned forward to kiss her, his lips had barely touched hers before she pulled herself away. He was very alluring she felt.

She had dated a few guys and they had kissed and held hands but even that tiny example of a kiss from Kyle was starting to put a chink in her armor of self control. "What's wrong Delilah? He asked with that deep sexy voice of his.

"You have some loose ends Kyle" she said staring straight ahead with her hands together in her lap. "I know, I'm going to take care of it as soon as I get home.

Do you believe me? I want YOU Delilah" he said reaching for her hand. He held her hand on the seat space between them, and they rode the rest of the way in silence.

It was weird for her because of all the guys who had ever pursued Delilah, Kyle was the only one who just rated her looks as "attractive". She felt average with him. The best compliment he ever gave her was regarding her long, pretty hair and her great sense of style. He felt she had too many clothes for one person. Now all of a sudden he was in love with her? Who wouldn't be flattered by a fine, no wait excuse me....... beautiful, intelligent and enchanting guy like Kyle acting like he had to have them? Was he really getting ready to dump someone he spent three years with for someone he only knew for three months? They were both arrogant, but he outdid her in that area as well as being smarter and better educated. He was the type who could lead and dominate her.

Lilah was walking in love now like an obedient servant, so for the first time in her life she was willing to be submissive to a man. She had always had her way with Kary, he was a strong man, he just enjoyed pleasing her.

Kyle was reminding her of Kary now the way he was bending over backwards trying to please her and cater to her. He still managed to let her know who the boss was whenever she would over step her bounds with him. When they pulled into Natalie's drive way, Kyle got out and walked her to the door. "I'm going to call you when I get home. Then we'll call HER on the three way. I want you to know I am for real." "You don't have to do it with me listening in Kyle", she said feeling guilty. She had accepted that she wanted him too, but she didn't like feeling responsible for what he was about to do. "I want you to be there, can I have a kiss?" He had these big ,beautiful eyes with long, thick lashes. His lips were full and rosy in color. Lilah just nodded her head answering yes.

That kiss was so warm and sensuous, she felt like she was melting and floating in his arms at the same time. If she wasn't certain how she felt before, she was now. He had done the deed within an hour later, and Lilah heard the girl tell Kyle if things didn't work out for him not to come crawling back to her. This conversation was different from the others they had on the phone for hours, because they were a couple now. It had gotten late but they still couldn't hang up just yet. He asked her what she was doing at that moment. "You tired baby?" he asked. "Yeah I got to work in the morning too." "It's already morning, lay down on the bed right now", he said. She laid on the bed while they talked some more. Twenty minutes later he asked, " What are you doing now?" "You told me to lay down", she said. "Oh my God!!" he yelled with a sense of excitement. "What?" Lilah thought something was wrong. "I can't believe you actually did what I told you to." Neither could she. "You're going to make a good wife." He had finally said goodnight or morning and Lilah went to sleep feeling like a character in a "happily ever after" story.

Kyle would come over to study and stay for dinner when Lilah wasn't working.

One night Natalie claimed she was too tired to drop him off and told him he could spend the night. Lilah always wondered did Natalie know what she was doing? Did she have any idea how hard Kyle was to resist, and now he was staying all night?! After as much bumping in grinding in their clothes coupled with kissing, as Lilah could stand... she went to bed leaving him on the sofa. It was so hard, she hadn't wanted anyone that bad or at all the way she wanted Kyle.

She had been celibate two whole years and content with it until now. His body had felt so good pressed into hers, she could feel his erectness. Making it even harder to leave him out there, but she did. The next morning Kyle had left with Natalie and she went to work.

All she could think about at work was how long it was going to be before she caved.

How long could they attempt to resist what was so powerfully strong between them like a moth to a flame? More importantly, how long did they have to?! He hadn't exactly proposed to her, but he was promising one. Things were happening so fast, she decided it was probably a good idea to put some space between them altogether. That night after Lilah had explained that she feared it was too much like a fairytale romance. That had a whirlwind effect, sweeping her off her feet. Kyle became desperate to keep his foot in the door. "Baby please don't do this, don't fight what's right!" he begged her.

"A few days apart won't kill us, it will only make us stronger. We'll still talk on the phone everyday", she cried, hoping he wasn't too disappointed. It was a challenge, something they both craved in life. "Okay I won't come over until next week, but I'll see you at church on Wednesday night." It was Sunday evening, so that felt long enough for Lilah, she agreed. "Okay Kyle, I love you." "I love you too", he said. The coming days were rough, but between Wednesday, when they sat together at church and hugged goodbye, the tension had really intensified for both. A week later, they were studying in the den, right outside

Delilah's bedroom in the basement. When all of a sudden, Kyle got unusually weird and uncomfortable.

Chapter Five

"Are you okay sweetheart?" She asked him. Not looking up from his bible he said, "I'll be okay". "Okay from what, what's bothering you Kyle?" Lilah asked concerned. "I'm trying my best to behave myself, but you entice me. Those pantyhose you're wearing are so sexy", he said biting his bottom lip and grabbing his crotch with both hands. "I'm sorry, I didn't mean to tempt you, I can change." Delilah hadn't realized how much her legs and paisley laced stockings were exposed, since she was wearing cropped pants below her calf. She had been sitting beside him with her legs crossed, swinging the elevated leg up and down while reading.

She got up to go to her room, she really didn't want to tempt Kyle. She felt if they finally did go too far, she would be responsible. He was more of a babe spiritually than she was, he had just got saved the day she met him at church. Totally unaware that she was the lamb and the wolf was waiting to prey on her, not pray with her. Delilah was in her room sitting on her bed wearing nothing but panties, trying to get a foot in some jogging pants when he let himself in. She was nervous instantly, she knew he wasn't looking to compromise.

He had stepped out of boundaries into her bedroom. "Kyle, what are you doing?" she asked. Afraid to swallow the lump in her throat for fear he might hear her heart beating rapidly. "I want to look at you, I won't touch you if you don't want me to." His eyes were big and kind of sad. Glazed over as if he was in pain over her. "I don't think we should be playing with fire this way", she said almost crying now. "I'm going to see eventually, I want to know what you look like naked when I go home tonight. If it will make you feel any better, I'll go first." He said pulling his shirt over his head and tossing it.

Then loosed his belt and unzipped so slowly she could hear the teeth of his zipper separating to the beats of her heart. She wasn't even looking at him, too afraid she'd like what she saw and ashamed. She could see enough from the corner of her eye, that he was bending over pushing his jeans down.

He walked over and stood directly in front of her. He was so close she could smell his flesh.... his meat. Trying to look away from him, he grabbed her face gently with one hand turning her face forward until her lips and nose almost brushed his erect penis. Lifting her chin he said, Delilah, look at me. Can't you see how much I want you?" "I can't Kyle", she cried softly. She didn't have to look to know she wanted him too. She knew she was about to surrender, but not without a fight.

"Open your eyes baby" he said in that deep sexy voice and breathing heavy.

She shook her head hysterically and pulled away, falling into her pillow crying harder. She heard him whisper, "It's okay, I'm pulling my pants back up." She kept her head buried into the pillow while the room had grown silent, she couldn't even hear him breathing anymore. He said he was leaving because he was embarrassed and that was the last time she heard his voice. Then she heard him again just as she was getting ready to raise up. "Will you at least look at me so I can see your face while I apologize?" It didn't seem like too much to ask considering she was acting like a scared little girl. She slowly rose up and turn her head even slower to look at him. Kyle was still standing there stark naked with an erection that would quit!

She was both shocked and amused by what she saw, his manhood had a curve that said, "Come hither" and it was very persuasive. Now that she was aroused, it was still hard to relax. He had seduced her in the cruelest way she thought. "It's your turn", he said as his eyes went from hers to her crotch.

"Kyle please" she begged him. "Stop Delilah, I'm going to marry you I promise.

What we are doing is not wrong, as long as we're getting married." He was on his knees now, pleading with his eyes for her to surrender. "Okay", she conceded taking her blouse and panties off. Her bra was always last, since she had a complex about being small busted. He stood her straight up and backed away from her to get a good look at her trembling body. This turned him on

even more. "Now lay down", he commanded. She did so in a defeated kind of body language. She watched him as he walked over to her, climbing on top of her without touching her. He kissed her lips and her erect nipples, then her belly.

He could tell she was scared and that excited him, so much his penis jumped tapping her on her stomach. With his eyes locked into hers, inhaling each breath she let out, he pierced her slightly then plunged into her without further pause until there was no space between them and nowhere else to go inside of her. She sighed with relief and pleasure, they both moaned in ecstasy, and then it was over. After he had thrust and grind her only about five times he exploded inside of her. It was too much, the excitement, the feel of her and the anticipation that led up to it. He pulled out of her and noticed she was ashamed again of what they'd done. He laid next to her real close writing the words, "I love you" on her belly with his finger, to reassure her she could trust him.

They kissed and held each other awhile and then she got up and left the room to take a shower. When he was dressed he came out of the room, it was an awkward moment for her. He told her everything was going to be alright and said goodnight. She went to bed after she realized he wasn't going to call.

She didn't think the worst, he probably was embarrassed about climaxing so soon.

Tomorrow would be soon enough for her, she was quite embarrassed herself.

Still, she couldn't wait to get inside his head to find out what his after thoughts were about that night. When she got home from work, she went straight to her room to call him. She had a surprisingly good day and felt she owed that to Kyle.

"Hello", Kyle answered in a dry tone. "Hi baby how are you?" she asked ignoring his aloofness. "I'm alright, listen I was going to call you, because I have something to tell you." By now she was starting to sense something was terribly wrong. "What is it Kyle?", she asked not really wanting an answer. "I made a mistake.... I don't love you." The sound of those words was so horrific all she could do was drop the phone and scream. "Noooooooooo!!!!"

She could hear him calling her and telling her not to cry. Some nerve he had, did he realize what she had compromised for him?! Now the very next day he's sorry, he don't love her?! He hoped they could still be friends because he thought she was a beautiful person(apparently on the inside), but she was not his "type".

He was going to try to get his EX back. He was the same pompous jerk who didn't give dark girls the time of day he always was. So why did he spend so much time and energy seducing Delilah? What was so special about her? He had really dumped

his EX, only to turn around and dump Lilah. Now he was still in love with the other girl, and worried his children might not be as gorgeous as he was if he married Delilah. Yes, he had the nerve to tell her all this, Negro Puhleeeease! Little did

Kyle know, Lilah would have three beautiful kids some years later that he himself had the pleasure of meeting. All he could say was, "Wow, you got some pretty kids girl!"

Poor Lilah felt so ugly and dirty that night. It wasn't so much that Kyle thought she was ugly, just not light enough for his liking. Devastated as she was, she was determined this was not happening to her. She been a lot of things in her life, but never been dumped before. Plus she was convinced she was in love with him, so she was willing to give him some time to realize what a mistake he was making.

She even begged him to let her visit, this was not like Lilah. She bowed before no man! She wasn't a chaser, she was a catcher. She had long vowed before she ever dated that she wasn't going to be ANYTHING like her mother when it came to men. Being strong was everything to her, so what was so special about Kyle? How

much pride and dignity was she willing to swallow? The things we do when we think somebody got more out of us than we got out of them.

He loved the humility she showed, so he told her to come over. When she got there though, he could barely look at her. He wasn't the same guy at all, though he tried to be polite. It was hard for him to keep being a jerk because she was all heart, innocence and naïve. Which kind of cornered him on his own turf. They went to his room where he attempted to explain some things to her. One thing he wasn't doing anymore was lying and giving her false hope. He didn't get the girl back and seemed bitter Lilah brought it up. "Listen, I want you but I don't love you", he said to her. She looked sad but understanding. Understanding that he wasn't going to get her in bed again just because he was being honest about only wanting sex.

Sitting on the edge of his bed, tears began to roll down his face. He then reached under the bed and grabbed a gun, putting it to his head. Delilah was stunned, bad as he hurt her she didn't want this. "What are you doing Kyle?!" she yelled in disbelief. "I'm never going to be able to forgive myself for what I did to you", he said, cocking the gun. "No Kyle, don't do this! I forgive you!" Lilah cried. He put the gun down sobbing and apologizing to her. He told her she was the best thing that ever happened to him and he could never be the man she deserved. Then he asked her to leave.

She ran out of the house crying, crying all the way back to Pastor Kilborn's church.

She found the pastor and Kyle's friend Cord talking in the pews. She pulled Cord to the side and asked him to go check on Kyle. Lilah went into the kitchen to tell Pastor's wife Annie what happened. Everything, how Kyle had played her and what he pulled today. While she was being consoled by Annie, Cord returned with Kyle.

When Lilah came out of the kitchen, Pastor was walking away from Kyle. He was just sitting there alone now. No expression, no sound....just tears. Pastor had really giving him a dose of tough love with some prayer. He and Natalie both had entrusted Kyle with Lilah, who was like a daughter to him. Even Cord was disappointed in him. His game had back fired, he had gone too far to hurt a harmless and good soul.

It wasn't until later Lilah would learn from his friend, that it was all over a bet.

Kyle was going to win no matter what, he was morally corrupted by his ego. His reputation was on the line too, so it was either his or hers. He couldn't have people thinking a woman resisted him. So he won the bet that he could get Lilah off the straight and narrow. Hmmph, she gave him credit though, she told everyone he deserved an Oscar for his performance. From the seduction right down to the so called suicide attempt. It wasn't long before Lilah was bouncing back and realizing she didn't love him either. Her own ego was in the way, she couldn't just concede without some satisfaction of seeing him suffer too. When everyone saw him as an evil, no good con artist, she was content to move on.

It didn't even bother her to see him anymore at church, of course everything that came out of his mouth was a lie now. He could tell he didn't matter to her anymore, and probably felt he was off the hook with the church because of it. The light was gone in Delilah's eyes now. She was damaged goods all over again. She still came to church, but if the devil could walk up in the church, chew you up and spit you out like that, what was the point of trusting anyone to protect you but yourself? This was Lilah's mentality now, this is the state Kyle's betrayal left her in. Somehow, somewhere and someway, she knew hell was going to catch up with Kyle and serve him well. She was cool with that, something had just gone terribly wrong with her heart and attitude though.

She was guarded, cold-hearted and unapproachable in a way that scared those close to her.

Her relationship with God was falling by the wayside, and the one she had with Natalie was coming to a head. She didn't have much to relate to living with Natalie that was black. No black people, or culture other than once a week at Pastor Kilborn's in the old neighborhood. On top of that, Natalie was firm as brick with her rules! Compromise was not an option! She couldn't watch shows like Good Times or even the Cosby Show. Couldn't listen to secular music, she longed for some Anita Baker and Sade. The only time she got to enjoy them was when she was with her younger friend Connie, who's mother was a good friend of Natalie's. Connie introduced Lilah to the Beastie Boys and Lilah shared Whodini in return. Lilah was 20 years old being treated like a child! Being told what she couldn't listen to or watch, when she paid room and board and out of zone fees when she called her Grandmother in the ghetto. It was too much, it wasn't like she was partying, drinking and smoking, she just liked a variety of music and wanted to watch some TV sometimes! Connie and her mom even tried to mediate some type of compromise

between them to keep Lilah from moving out, but Natalie wouldn't bend. Delilah packed her things and returned home.

Pastor chastised Natalie that Lilah had moved out and turned bitter towards God because of her choke hold. For giving her "meat" when she was not ready for solids spiritually speaking instead of giving her milk and weaning her away from the worldly things gradually. She had given up so much of her own free will, was still a good Christian and staying out of trouble. "If they were so worried about her, what the hell were they doing when "Kyle the K 9" was going for her jugular?!" she thought.

Chapter Six

Stepfather was gone now. He had finally packed up and moved on. I think that was a punch in the gut for her mother. That after twenty plus something years of going through hell with this man, he left without notice. He had done her a favor for sure. In all of her self righteous pride, she had to tell everybody she had thrown him out and finally gotten rid of him. That she was glad he was gone. Yeah, right, she had Delilah's sympathy. She knew it had to be hard to be left by a drug addict when you thought you were high and mighty. Whatever she wanted to believe was fine with Delilah, except she knew her mother was no more convinced than she was. She wasn't truthful about herself or her life. She down played anyone or anything that threatened her image. Mainly Lilah, who had to be a sick, messed up child by choice or birth because she or nothing she chose to do or not do ,could have affected or made Delilah who or what she was. She simply had no fault in it.

Delilah was who her mother needed everybody to believe she was, psychotic, dramatic and overly emotional for no apparent reason. Delilah had immersed herself

into her work. Two jobs she was holding to keep herself occupied and away from men. She helped her mother with food and ends. Besides her younger brother and sister, there were two other children there now. Her mother's youngest sister had just abandoned her kids, they seemed pretty messed up by it too. They were her cousins and as detached as

Delilah had grown accustomed to being emotionally, she felt sorry for them. She use to babysit them when she was still in high school and their mom was like a goddess to Lilah then. She was beautiful like the model Beverly Johnson. Delilah only hoped she would be as pretty one day. She had seen a side to her Aunt she didn't like. She was vain, evil and self centered, but she could also be nice to Lilah and her sister. They liked her a lot growing up still.

Now she was on drugs and acting a fool. Another role model had died on Lilah in a sense. First Pastor had been sexing his assistant and then married her after being busted by the congregation. She had lost some respect for him, but not love. They had still done a great deal for her in different ways, no matter what they had done in their personal lives. They were good to her. They were human, they had infirmities just like everybody else. The simply needed what they had given, love and understanding, Lilah concluded. Natalie was done with them, she had stoned them. Anyway, Lilah decided her mother was giving her sister that love and understanding, even though she took everything and everyone for granted. Here we were struggling to feed and care for her children who didn't seem to understand why they didn't have a mother or father now. Their father had passed and mama had done lost her mind and gone buck wild.

Shortly after her twenty-first birthday, Delilah's mom would drop a bomb on her. A bomb meaning it took her long enough to do it, because it certainly wasn't a surprise. She had given up on ever getting the truth out of her about her biological father. There had been rumors about him, but her mother denied them all. Lilah was told her stepfather was her real dad, but she knew he wasn't. He had even told her he wasn't. So why did she feel so compelled to tell the truth now? It looked like she didn't have anything to lose now from where Lilah was standing. Even if her father had been dead since she was a baby, she still had a right to know about him. She had a right to know who SHE was if not him! Especially since Step dad obviously didn't want to be burdened with her. To be in a family that you loved, but didn't act like, think like or look like was tough. You needed to understand where it came from just to survive the alienation. Turned out, there was somebody looking for Lilah. Her paternal grandmother had run in to her mother before. Seeing it as a blessing and wanting to re-unite with Lilah. Plans and promises were made, but oh yeah, Step dad was more important! She had covered her tracks pretty good keeping Delilah's paternal relatives a step behind when ever they came close to finding her. Chance meetings with her grandmother were unpredictable to her mother's dismay. Grandmother had some ammunition this time. She said, "I know where she works, her half sister found her. If you don't tell her about me, I will. I want to get to know here before I leave this world. I've already missed so much." So in finally learning all of this, Lilah was not so much pleased as she was relieved. She had finally gotten official confirmation that Step dad was indeed NOT her father. She didn't have conflict with him anymore, she just always knew there wasn't any blood let alone a bond between them. His behavior towards her would have been so much easier to accept under the truth. Maybe even explained his behavior despite how unacceptable and unexcused it was.

She wanted to understand and see where her looks and traits came from. She needed a few days to get herself together before calling the number her mother gave her. She had no idea what to do, say or feel, it was all surreal. It was easy though, Grandma was cool and it felt familiar talking to her on the phone. When Delilah got to her grandmother's house, she was relieved her grandmother was so pleased with her. She didn't see any resemblance between them right away, but Grandma knew she was her only child's daughter. She had seen Delilah before, twice. She said, "Your mama brought you by and my son held you, and you both just stared at each other. You looked at him like , "who is this man looking just like me?" she chuckled. She had so much to tell Lilah about her father and Grandfather(both deceased), and she was eager to hear all of it. She only had baby pictures of him, girlfriends and friends had stolen all of his pictures as a young man. Her mother had told her once, now that she had told her the truth. That her father was a womanizer and probably would have been a horrible father to Delilah?! Delilah's father didn't try to work things out with her mom , so of course he didn't want her either. So of course he was bad for Lilah and she had the right to decide who was better suited. Why did she even bother to tell the man he had a daughter then? Why didn't she just never look back? The second time Grandma would see Lilah was at her son's funeral, after that she never saw Lilah again. She had been hearing that somebody saw her somewhere as a child, but they could never find her when they looked again in that area or place.

Delilah recalled times when people had just stared at her like they knew her and her mother would suddenly get anxious and in a rush to get moving. Her mom knew these people but she didn't. Delilah had learned that her mother wasn't looking out for no one but herself. She didn't need her grandmother to tell her this, she had been living it all her life. Lilah had found a piece of herself in a big way. Grandma was a small framed woman. Delilah didn't have big bones and thickness like her mother's side the way her sister did. She was tall and slender, but she had an athletic build. Her grandmother was genuine too, she spoke her mind and she was free. Something else Lilah could relate too. As close as Lilah was to her other grandmother, this was different. It was different in the way she could just be free to say "fuck it" if she wanted to and not feel guilty.

She was jazzy and cool , like a female version of Frank Sinatra and Dean Martin.

Witty, charming, funny and tough as nails. Delilah knew she was in the right place now. There was no doubt that this is where she came from. Grandma Hattie just stared at Delilah in awe that first night. Kept telling her how much she looked like her dad. That she even had the same expressions and looked like he did when he was sleepy. "The eyes" she said, "they are hauntingly the same." She stayed the night and was going to meet the woman her dad would marry, whom he had two children with the next day. To her surprise, she had already met the siblings, they went to high school together.

The sister had approached Delilah once in high school after several friendly encounters. She asked Lilah,"What's your mother's name?" Delilah felt comfortable enough talking to the girl, so she answered, "Pilar". "What's your father's name?" Wondering why she was so interested in her family, Lilah proceeded to see where this was going. "Cleo, why?" "That's not your father's name." the girl said. Lilah laughed because even though that was exactly what she wanted to hear, she had been smoking marijuana and thought the girl must've been too. She was concerned that Lilah wasn't taking her seriously, she was trying to tell her something. "Your father's name is Julian, you and I have the same father." "Okay, see you later", Lilah said laughing and shaking her head as she walked away. She assumed the girl must have had her confused with someone else. Later that evening when her buzz had worn off, she realized this girl may have been telling the truth. She told her mother about it and asked who they might have been. She said nothing, except it was a lie. The girl never got a chance to approach Lilah again, she dropped out right after that incident.

Now she wondered if her new sister had assumed she was the reason for her disappearing act. The next time Lilah would see her sister she was working two jobs at the mall. She remembered her from school and was glad to see her. She didn't say anything but hello to Lilah this time. One of Lilah's jobs she worked with her sister's cousin. This time the cousin was asking the same questions regarding Lilah's parents. The brother and Lilah caught the bus home from school a lot. They use to laugh and joke around. She was so mad when she realized how cute he was that she could have dated him. Only he knew she was his sister, he just never said anything. He seemed to just want to hang around her without freaking her out the way the sister had done unintentionally. They were a pair of good looking kids too.

They had this gorgeous straight black hair like Mexicans and pretty caramel complexions. Her mother had told her, just recently, that her father had the straightest, silkiest hair for a black boy. He was black as night too. This would explain why Lilah was so dark, because her mother wasn't dark.

Their mother was as happy as they were to meet Lilah. She had recalled a time when they all met up in a convenience store by chance. Lilah was with her Mom and Kary(one of the times she got anxious to leave) that day, she vaguely remembered.

For the first time in her life, Lilah was the center of the family's attention and affection. Even though she felt she was getting along with both Tiffani and Romez, Grandma's attention and preference caused a sudden resentment in Tiffani. Sadly, the resentment was for Delilah, who actually didn't like the way Grandma had left Tiffani out. She didn't understand what was happening between her and Tiff. She and Romez continued to bond while Tiff silently grew bitter behind a facade. She started scheming and plotting against Lilah, suddenly it was war!

Sometimes we try to bring certain chemicals, elements and ingredients together that simply won't mix. They either separate, dissolve or cause complete disaster.

Chapter Seven

Delilah didn't want to lose her new sister, I mean they had just met really. She didn't know what exactly was wrong , but she knew something wasn't right. She got her sister a job where she worked so they could spend more time together. Tiff had a little girl, who was Lilah's first niece. The job didn't permit them to spend too much time because Lilah had been promoted to office manager. They saw even less of each other at work after a while. Tiff invited her over after work one day, and Lilah was happy to accept. Only to find out it was a set up, and that was the day Lilah would learn Tiff had a vendetta with her. Romez defended Lilah from Tiff's unjust and cruel behavior. It had gotten so bad the argument turned into a brawl between them. Out of spite against Romez for doing the right thing, Tiff exposed his personal business. It was obvious she had a problem with him being gay. He seemed to think it would make Lilah love him less too, she wasted no time assuring him it did not matter to her. He was her brother and a human being. He definitely had a heart, which was more than she could say for Tiff right now. Delilah was both hurt and angry. She had no idea Tiff felt that way about her. She was if anything, the complete opposite of what Tiff accused her of being. Fake, stuck up and two-faced. "Where was this girl getting this from?" she thought. Her own mother had referred to her as a evil, jealous bitch that night.

This pleased Delilah's mother more than she sympathized with her pain. She wanted to be right about her paternal relatives, that they probably weren't worth knowing. There's a rotten egg in every family. It didn't mean her and Romez had to suffer just because Tiff had gone mad.

Prior to the brawl incident, Tiff had introduced Lilah to Ellis. She had been talking to him on the phone weeks before meeting him in person. They had hit it off to a good start, but when Ellis heard about the fight he felt compelled to tell Lilah something even more shocking. He had a part in her sister's revenge, he was suppose to seduce her and dump her (the way Kyle had done), but instead he fell in love with her. Tiff wasn't too happy about that, her plan was backfiring. The more she tried to curse Lilah the more it seemed she was blessing her. Delilah had gone through celibacy another year or so before Ellis. She could only hope she was wiser in choosing him as she had been in the past. This would be the man she conceived those three beautiful children with. Delilah's younger sister Shai was a mother now. Something about her nephew really went deep, she could never get to know her niece now that her other sister was always out to get her. She had to let them both go.

The time she spent with her nephew made her reconsider Ellis' request to have children with her. He had a nephew also, and he was really good with him. Delilah really enjoyed her life and her freedom, she couldn't really see herself as a mother and was afraid she wouldn't be a good mother not having a good example set before her. She noticed that she had only seen Tiff's daughter a few times. That was because

Tiff was always clubbing and hanging out and her niece was with her father's family a lot. Though Lilah loved children and had spent a lot of time with her own baby brother and taking care of him, she was more afraid of failing than having been failed. Little Ricky was like sunshine and a big part of Lilah wished he was hers. Delilah and Ellis moved in their first apartment together and a few months later she was with child. When tiff heard about it she was pissed.

You'd think she would have checked herself by now, they hadn't spoken to her in months, Delilah or Ellis. The phone rang at five AM one morning, and it was a drunken Tiff. "Why'd you have to get her pregnant, you know I want you!" she yelled into the phone. "Go to sleep Tiff, you're drunk", Ellis replied hanging up the phone. There was only one down side to Ellis at this point, he was a drug dealer.

I guess you could say a pimp too, with desperate women lavishing him with gifts for any attention they could get from him. Lilah could not get with that and told him she was going to walk away from it all. He stopped hustling and got a job. Once their life together had started, Ellis found it hard to settle down. Always in the streets, jumping from one job to another. Finally he demanded he was going to hustle again and that everything was going to be fine.

It wasn't so much the danger of it that bothered her as the fact that most of his "business associates" were gay. Lilah always had a bad feeling about it but wanted to believe it was just business, nothing more. She was alone in their apartment so much during her last trimester, that her mother suggested she come and stay there. She knew Lilah had to be scared being this was her first child and all. Ellis visited a lot, bringing her whatever she needed. He was buying so much stuff for the baby ,it looked like he was preparing for the Messiah. Such beautiful baby furniture, Lilah felt they had a to find a house to match it. Lilah knew that this baby meant a lot to Ellis. She had caught him flirting a few times, along with her suspicions about his gay friends, but she wasn't insecure at all. She had grown up since Kary and Kyle. Her heart wasn't in this the way she had put herself out there in the past. She was still in it to win it though, She didn't like wasting her time on things and people she felt were getting no where.

Ellis was a good man, her mother and family had taken a liking to him. Her mother liked him better than she liked her, Lilah would joke with Ellis. Ellis was handsome with big dimples and big hazel eyes. He had pretty teeth too, tall and slim. He had a compassionate heart and was very romantic. Delilah didn't even know what an orgasm was until she met Ellis. It wasn't long before Lilah would discover something she really hated about Ellis, his lack of strength and ability to stay consistent. He whined and argued about how hard everything was, always telling her she had it easy because she was a woman. Almost as if he wished he was one. They started to argue and fight a lot when he realized she was losing respect for him. He loved her, but he also resented her. She didn't appreciate being a crutch for a weak person. She didn't mind helping him up when he had fallen, but the point was for him to get the hell back up and stay up. He couldn't seem to do that after

Eileena was only a year old. He had done so much for her and his daughter, that picking up the slack seemed like a small price to pay for keeping her family together. He was drinking and cheating, (with men and women) and getting violent. He may have even been doing drugs then, who knows? While pregnant with the second child, Ellis had slammed Lilah so many times, it was a miracle she hadn't miscarried. He had never done such evil things to her before. Then when E.J. Was born, he wouldn't even hold him. This infuriated Lilah because she knew he had doubts about E.J. Being his son. The nerve of this unproductive brother with no job accusing her of cheating and having baby by somebody else. Who would have gladly rescued her from this trip down hell's kitchen she was in. Delilah was faithful and steadfast in her commitment to him.

She knew Ellis was turning his guilt of cheating and having another kid on the way on to her. That baby was born a week after E.J., another boy.

They struggled to maintain their family, despite the other child. After seeing E.J. Change and grow, and that he had his dimples, complexion and smile he was convinced. Delilah was not staying around if he didn't snap out of his bull. She watched him with E.J. Until she was certain he was sincere. No child of hers was going to be abused in her care. He still favored Eileena though, you could tell she was the apple of his eye. This left Lilah feeling obliged to do a little extra for E.J. Who needed male bonding and adored his father. Thank God it wasn't as obvious to E.J. Then, Ellis loved children and was kind to E.J., he was just sort of distant with him. By the time the children were three and four, she had baby Endya.

Endya was a sight for sore eyes, boy was she a beauty. She looked more like Ellis than the other two. Where did she come from was the question. During the whole pregnancy she pondered for answers. She and Ellis had split up a year earlier. She was going to school and working full time, leaving no room for romance. Ellis cared for the kids while she was gone and left when she returned. One night he had cooked dinner and served her when she got home from work. He offered to pour her a drink while she studied for an exam. She started to feel exhausted and turned in while Ellis stayed up with the kids. When she awoke the next morning, she felt a dampness all up the back of her gown and turned to find Ellis half dressed lying next to her. "What are you doing?!" she yelled in disbelief and disgust. "Nothing, I'm leaving" he said anxiously leaving the room. A month later she had to quit her job at the Doctor's office because she was so sick all the time. She found out she was pregnant a week after that. Ellis until this day, won't admit he drugged her and had sex with her that night, and God only knows how many times. Endya was proof he had violated her, she was the only thing good that came from it. There was no denying his splitting image. Endya was the female version of Ellis. She was what the pretty boy was as a girl. To Ellis, she was his ticket back into Lilah's life. She assured him there was no way in hell, especially now that she knew what he was capable of in desperation. After two years with no success at getting his family back, he married his other son's mother. With Delilah's blessing I might add. Realizing Ellis was not the one for her, was one of the reasons she had gone back to school. She had realized love wasn't what kept her with Ellis, family, dedication and lust was. Lust is desire, Lilah's desire was to succeed. To keep her family together, but not at the expense of her own happiness.

She wasn't telling him he couldn't see his children though. They loved their dad,but Ellis just dropped from their lives in a flash. He spiraled down a self destructive path of drugs. At times, his kids wouldn't hear from him or see him for a year or more. Delilah sympathized with Ellis and her children. She would even try to help him get on his feet even though she had moved on and he was married. He seemed to be escaping his marriage and his life through drugs. Lilah and Ellis were bound by their children. She had forgiven him for all the betrayals, assaults and violations. They were past the past, dealing with the present, but certain there was no future. Delilah was big in that way, she was a giant ball of strength and resilience. She could see the good in people when no one else could.

Ellis was not happy with his life and his choices. It was like he was trapped inside of himself, even dying inside of himself. There was hope, but Ellis was the one who had to believe in himself, to save himself. He struggled for over a decade and today, one can only hope he has finally defeated his demons and got a sure grip and control in his life. He seems to be doing well for himself these days. His relationship with E.J. Remains unstable, but Lilah encourages her son to forgive and beware. Not to be bitter as she was with her own mother reminded of past indiscretions on top of present ones. "It's not your fault if you forgive people but they never change. If they keep doing the same things over and over to you in different ways and days, it's still the same old shit. You can only change how you allow them to affect you and if you decide altogether they're just not worth it at all, well then there it is" she would tell E.J.

Tiff had been trying to mend fences with Lilah over the years. She hadn't met any of the children and had given birth to a son the same year Eileena was born. Ellis advised Lilah against reconciling with her sister. Since he had known her since they were kids, Lilah felt he had the better judgment. Yet, Lilah felt it was time to bury the hatchet. She loved her half sister just as much as she did a whole sister.

Besides, Shai had done some scandalous stuff to her too. Why forgive one when you can't forgive the other? That just wasn't Lilah, it may have been a mistake to forgive Tiff but she needed to try. Their Grandmother had passed away when Eileena was a baby. She didn't even tell anybody she was sick. That was something else Lilah had in common with her. She kept her pain and suffering to herself most of the time. When you have suffered ordeals like rape and abuse and no one rescued you or answered your screams, you grow accustomed to dealing with things on your own. She'd tell people she was fine even if she wasn't. She believed she could be if she said she was. Grandma didn't have to die alone, but she understood. She could see herself doing the same, wanting her children to just enjoy their last days without pity and sorrow. Delilah's motto was ,"Love me as much as you can while you can, cause when

I'm gone it won't matter". So as long as Lilah was breathing, anyone who wanted to make things right with her could do so, but they had to understand she wasn't trying to go in circles and find herself repeating the same old mistakes over and over even if they was happy with that. You had to be sincere, she could tell when her time was being wasted. At some point enough has really got to be enough.

If you were shamming, you were shamming yourself because she was dealing with you on a superficial level after having learned what you're about, but yes YOU had to be sincere to even get that now.

Believe or not, Lilah's step dad had even made amends with her by the time she'd had Eileena. Forgiving somebody is one thing, but when they find the courage to ASK you for it?! Whew, that is something else! That's a paradise that warms your soul like the sight of a sunset on a summer night hitting calmed ocean waves. It's like you become even freer. He had done what he needed to do for his own freedom and gave Lilah a little more of it at the same time. At least maybe he slept a little better at night, had a little more peace. That's more than her mother was willing to do for Lilah or herself. She didn't owe Lilah an apology for nothing and didn't mind telling her so. She'd been around the mountain with this woman too many times already for one lifetime as far as she was concerned. Too many because through it all, Pilar's heart never seems to change or at least the value she likes to hold Lilah to. She even brought that same discrimination she subjected Lilah to onto her children. They weren't good enough , or as good as Shai's kids because they were Lilah's. This helped

Lilah realize what the core of her problem was and where it came from......her mother. The root of the evil, the very tree she came from, had branched out all over her life.

Chapter Eight

Pilar wanted or needed Lilah to doubt Cleo's sincerity. That he couldn't possibly be feeling any remorse about the past with the exception that, his nephew had sexually assaulted her. Pilar believed that the guilt of those tragedies ate at his conscience enough to make him sorry he didn't prevent them, she just couldn't grasp the fact that he was done lying and denying everything the way she still was. It's got to be hard defending someone and siding with them against a child for years and then watch them beat you to admitting they were wrong and saying sorry. Too stubborn and foolish to admit wrong doing without having an ulterior motive. This is who she is, if it isn't something in it for her she doesn't see the point. She certainly never lets one hand do something the other can't see. You can bet she has a receipt somewhere. There are people who have life insurance to ensure their loved ones are cared for or properly buried in the event that should happen. Pilar has insurance on children and grand children as if she actually expects them to die before her so she can reap an investment. Half of whom she didn't give the time of day and thought she was too good for.

Guilty people are paranoid and suspicious naturally. At first Cleo was innocent and could do no wrong, or it was the drugs he was doing fault and not HIS for doing them. Now, he was lying and up to no good. According to Cleo, there was a time when he adored Lilah so much it upset Pilar . He believed Lilah was his daughter at first because she looked like his mother to him. Who had passed away when Lilah was a baby. Pilar and Cleo had separated and he would keep Lilah at his place for days where she had everything a little girl could want. He would wash her hair and try to braid it. Lilah had stolen yet another man's affections from Pilar. She had punished Julian by taking Lilah away from him and passing her off as Cleo's child because he moved on. Delilah was obviously a constant reminder of her father's infidelities and cruelty as it was. Still, she could use her to snare another man. Pilar is good at using people against one another. Everybody in some way or another, is just a pawn in her game. A bigot who feels she's in a position to judge the world according to her theories and philosophies. By the time Lilah was four, it was painfully obviously to Cleo, that his life was a complete lie. Once his own daughter was born and having met Lilah's father once, Cleo turned on Lilah. Having shared Pilar's resentment for Julian for pulling a switch blade on him in an attempt to see Lilah, they both targeted the only person they could with this resentment, Lilah. Julian was gone but lived through her.

Pilar didn't mind Lilah's suffering one bit as long as she had a man. It was the price she paid for her lies and deception. To give him his own children and let him mistreat hers. She suffered too though. One: For being a selfish fool and two: Cleo was getting the best of her by using and abusing her. Too busy trying to keep and please him at any cost. This is why no one was paying attention when his already full grown nephew tore into Lilah like a lion on a gazelle. A predator always watches to see what's being neglected for his delight. It is said that animals don't have morals, but even they protect their young better than some humans. In all retrospect, Lilah believed Cleo was sincere, in fact today she knows he is. He has never fallen back into his old ways with her....not once to this day. The man could look her in the eye and say he was sorry AND that he loved her! She could see the pain in his eyes I want to comfort him.

She told him one day accompanied by his sister, to let go of the past. That he didn't have to apologize every time he saw her, it had become a constant upon every approach with her. "All is forgiven, I'm okay and I want you to be okay too. I know in my heart if you could go back and do it all over again you'd do it differently. Instead, you have changed the future. You've made it easier for you and I to be free." she told him. It was hard for Cleo to be free though, but Lilah was certain those were other demons that didn't concern her haunting him. He was always asking for money but hey he was an addict! That too was a demon in his life but he had heart and humility, now all he needed was faith. She didn't have any good memories of her own with Cleo as a child, but she had some profound ones as an adult. "At least he won't die not having done right by her", she thought.

She and her sister Shai had been going through some hard core feuds over the years too. She was doing exactly what Mama had been doing right in front of them growing up, letting a man get between her and her family. Mama had reaped what she sowed and didn't like it one bit. It finally looked like Pilar hated somebody else more than she hated Lilah. That's because Shai was the apple of Pilar's eye and Shai worshiped at the throne of Ricky. Pilar had the nerve to say, "And the child you favor the most, is the one that turns against you", through big sobs to Lilah. Yes she had plenty of nerves then and even more today. Lilah's fallouts with Shai weren't due to this, even though she told Shai she was wrong for raising a brick to their mother. She certainly didn't deserve that, not from her anyway. They were because Ricky enjoyed the show Shai put on for him so much his ego inflated way beyond tolerable circumstances. Lilah did well to get along with this punk for her sister's sake as long as she did. She may have enjoyed the way he made her mother miserable secretly, but she'd never let him disrespect her the way Shai did. He had to keep it within bounds. She certainly didn't enjoy him flirting with her or the extremes of his advances. Until this day you can bet Shai believes the flirtations were mutual. That's the type of ignorant bliss she needs to live in to justify still being with him. She may have stopped letting him force her to choose him over her family, but it's her own choice to sugar coat the truth and rationalize his behavior for her satisfactory. "She needs to believe what she needs to believe", Lilah concluded. She has had to share responsibility with him for something that was beneath her, just to have peace with her sister. He branched out all over the place just like Cleo did, in and out of the family flirting and willing to commit incest. While these women sat in their miserable, ignorant bliss hating on Lilah for daring to call them out and being strong enough to deal with it head on.

These men were victims too. They weren't with women who allowed them to be men. They had ridden their Mama's skirts the first half of their lives and now caught on to their new Mama's skirts for the rest of it. They were controlling weaker subjects and wouldn't have been as effective as men running things in a more challenging relationship. This is why Lilah and Ellis were over, she knew he was still a boy (or a girl), and she needed a man or nobody at all. Pilar and Aunt Babe always encouraged Lilah to stay with Ellis. "He's a good man , they all cheat. He takes care of his family, that's what matters. He loves you as much as he's capable". She would have long been gone if not for their so-called counseling. They just enjoyed seeing her miserable as they were. I know this because when they saw how good she was doing without him and after making several inquiries as to whether she still wanted him, finding that she was so over him and beyond... they didn't seem happy or proud of her at all. She had managed to do what they couldn't. Delilah wasn't afraid to accept defeat and step into the unknown. To see what was on the other side of a door. Her reasoning was, "If I'm not happy on this side, let's see what's on the other side." What have you got to lose?!

Delilah remained strong as a single mother who was dedicated to bringing her children up with love and good values. She took them to church, they did things as a family like shopping, movies, restaurants and enjoying each other at home with close friends. She didn't have any serious relationships after Ellis for a few years. She was good about spacing time between relationships. Giving herself time to self reflect and grow into the next. Her children were her life and she got lost in her duty as a mother. She wouldn't meet anyone who could hold her attention until Seth. It wasn't love at first sight either. He ended up being

Delilah's first TRUE love, making Kary look like puppy love. She had no idea what loving a man from your heart was like until Seth arrived on the scene. She had been in control of her heart for so long, she could not imagine what was about to happen to it. Even when she got emotional her heart hadn't been penetrated. Like I said, he didn't make her eyes leap out of head but he was cute. He was kind of nerdy looking. He wore nice thin framed spectacles, had curly hair with a side part which Lilah felt was out dated. His dress was preppy, and on the nautical side and he drove a nice spots car. It was his approach that got her attention, he was a gentleman. One who appeared flabbergasted by her. That became even more of a compliment later when Lilah learned he lived amongst celebrities and the "beautiful people". She was calling her children in for dinner and picking their toys up from the lawn when he spotted her. He turned the corner and came back, got out of his car and introduced himself. Instead of calling her over to his car like the "hoods" do. He greeted her with a hand shake, and impeccably proper English.

She told him her nick name, "That is not your name, I would like to know the full name of the beautiful lady that stands before me", he demanded ever so confidently. She laughed at him and said "Delilah" mockingly of his demeanor, still not fully cooperating. He asked of she was married before leaving her with a number to reach him. He said he was only visiting in town but would like to take her out. That was cool, again she was quite casual and not looking for anything serious.

He seemed harmless and she wasn't threatened by him in nay way. She knew he was an intellectual which impressed her, but she wasn't worried about wanting him for keeps. They talked on the phone and made a date. He picked her up and they went Downtown. Her last date there had been with Kary, ten years earlier. They walked along side the river hand in hand, with him still staring at her like she was just the prettiest thing he'd ever seen. They found a spot where they would lean against the rails and stare out at the water and talk.

"So what made you want to go out me?" she asked. "You're pretty and you have great legs", he answered. "Wow, those must be rare assets" she responded with sarcasm in her voice. Feeling slightly intimidated by her, Seth explained, "No but it really made me curious as to what your rare assets might be." "Uh oh, he's smooth and quick with a comeback", Lilah thought. She smiled to ease his tension and assure him he was on the right track. Something she rarely did. She liked to keep them guessing. "I have three children you know?" she was upping the ante now. "Yes is their Dad around?" he asked. "Off and on. He's married now. Do you have any kids?" "No, not married yet", he answered. "Hmmm, strong family values too", she thought. A red Porsche had stopped behind them where two guys sat and appeared to just be staring at her. She didn't recognize the passenger and couldn't see the driver and found herself disgusted by their rudeness. "Do you know them" Seth asked. "No, you want to go somewhere else?" Before Seth could answer, the driver had gotten out of the car and was coming toward them. It was Kord to Delilah's surprise. Kyle's friend who went to Pastor Kilborn's church. He was the one who told Kyle what a jerk he was for following through on that bet. "Kord?!" Lilah yelled running into his arms as he lifted her up off the ground, swinging her around in excitement. "Oh my God, I can't believe it!" realizing she had abandoned Seth who looked like he was going to go off any minute, Lilah led Kord over to Seth and introduced them. "This is Kord, we went to church together", Seth shook his hand looking relieved that it wasn't a long lost EX. "Do you still go to church there?" Lilah asked. "Sometimes when I'm in town, I'm a pilot in the Air Force. Pastor showed me a photo of your kids, they're beautiful!" "Thank you, do you have any yet?" "Yeah, I got twin girls. I got married!" "Oh congratulations Kord, I'm glad things are going so well for you." "You too baby, and you're still fine. Let me get out of your way. It was good meeting you." he said turning to Seth and placing Lilah's hand in his. "You too", Seth said.

Lilah and Seth proceeded on their date, talking over dinner. In a moment of silence between them, Seth started laughing then shook his head. "Mmph, mmph , mmph", he said. "What?" Lilah asked. "You got niggas pulling over in Porsches and shit." Lilah couldn't believe her ears! Seth had cursed and sounded like a regular ghetto boy. He was jealous of someone she had known longer than him but never dated. "His ego shineth through", she teased. She knew it was the fact that Kord's car was nicer and he was cooler. Kord wasn't good looking but he was tall to Lilah's liking. Seth was average height but in great shape, he had served in the marines for five years. It pleased her that he felt it was going to be a challenge to keep her attention directed towards him. The night just got more exciting and unpredictably adventurous from there. After that night, if he wasn't visiting he was on the phone with her. He spent a lot of time on his computer, but she had to be on the phone so he knew what she was doing. Although she enjoyed Seth's company, she still wasn't feeling any thing for him.

He was really good with the kids and you could tell he's make a great father and husband, but things just seemed fine the way they were for Lilah. He catered to her the way Kary had, in fact that's who he reminded her of. The fact that she felt secure with him, like he had her back through thick and thin caused her to give him a whole hearted try. She knew he was into her. The thing was, he was only visiting. He had a life and career progressing in sunny California. One night while on the phone, Seth asked Lilah a question that caught her off guard. "When are you going to give me some?" "What?' Lilah asked embarrassingly. "I'm serious, I have been a complete gentleman. I really like you and I want you, but I'm not sure if you like me enough" He explained. "It's not that I don't like you, I do. You are going back to California, I need to think about this some more." "I understand, it's not like a fling to me though. I think we could work something out", Seth said. The next evening Lilah invited Seth over after the children had gone to bed. They made love for the first time and it was definitely a new experience. One she would cherish in years to come, it was that special for her. She still wasn't sure she was in love yet, but he was and didn't hide it. He was so into her, he would dread going to work in the morning.

When Opposites Attract by De Layna Starr Brady

When opposites attract

It's like learning something new and different.

It makes it seem and feel so special,

in the beginning.

When opposites attract

It's like a slow and curious journey

It's scary, exciting and complicated,

In the end.

Chapter Nine

Seth was so in love with Lila, he was offended she hadn't introduced him to her family yet. Mainly her Mother, who at the time had started dating again and was getting along with Lilah for the moment it seemed. Lilah had come a long way by herself. Nice duplex, fully furnished with all new pieces. Her sister Shai had been back at home with their mother, new boyfriend but on the verge of going back to Ricky. She had explained to Seth she needed to be sure they had something lasting going on between them first. The truth was, it wasn't the traditional honor he thought it was, at least it wasn't for Lilah. She didn't care what her mother thought of him, she knew he was a good guy so that's all that mattered. Her mother didn't think she deserved anyone decent anyway. Only Shai deserved such a man. After Seth had given her an engagement ring, she made the introduction. He had already moved to her state by then, working with his cousin's husband. Lilah had confessed to Seth that she did love him. He loved her back and she knew this from his actions which speaks louder than words any day.

After being certain she was sincere, he declared his love for her in words making it official. As if the proposal wasn't enough. They moved in together and she spent a lot of time with his sister Carla who had two sons. Lilah really enjoyed having Carla in her life, but after awhile the consistent visits made her feel smothered. She didn't intend to hurt feelings by saying so, but as mad as Seth got about it, she began to think Carla was her babysitter. Was she keeping watch for Seth while he worked and went back to California to work as an actor? An extra was more like it. He was visible but silent in all of his roles or parts, which was a start. He had gone and jumped the gun that he was just an accredited actor as Denzel Washington. Bragged to everybody he knew and didn't know and they all thought he was a joke. It got to be embarrassing for her. He started having fits and threatening to leave her, claiming she was jealous of him and wasn't acting like the strong secure woman he fell in love with. She loved Seth, but he needed a reality check and she didn't mind giving him one. She told him to do what he had to and started looking through her little black book. He wouldn't bulge, he even missed a few auditions and stayed at home more. Pilar and Shai didn't seem to like Seth much, I'm sure they thought he was an arrogant jerk. He could be, but Lilah knew how to maneuver around that and bring him back down to earth. They had also mentioned to Lilah that he acted like they were her servants instead of family. He would tell Lilah to call them to take her shopping and run her errands when he wasn't available. Even though he offered to pay them, they were insulted, especially Pilar. "I'm not your chauffeur, who does he think he is?!" she once snapped. "A good man who offers to pay my family to help me out and you're offended? You have taken me to the store many times for nothing at all, now it's an insult to be offered gas money? Or is it the fact that I actually have someone like that?" Lilah thought. They just couldn't stand how good she had it WHEN she had it good. Seth was a great father figure to the kids. By the way, the man could cook!

The time he spent further instilling good values in those kids, spending time with them, showing them love and providing for them was really mind blowing for Lilah. Unexpectedly, Ellis' father passed on. Lilah was getting the kids ready for the funeral, she hadn't even considered going even though she was once apart of the family. She was with Seth now and a part of his family. Seth came in that morning with a condolence card. "Here, I got this for you to take with you to the funeral", he said. She was so by his consideration for others. "I'm not going baby. But that was really sweet of you." "No, you should go, I'm sure he would want you to be there. Go say good bye to his father." Something about a confident man was very sexy to Lilah, she said okay, but she couldn't wait to get back home to her man. Especially with Ellis' family constantly acting like her and Ellis were still together when his wife is glued to his side the entire time. They just refused to see the woman, no wonder she hated Lilah. Ellis asked if the kids could stay after the funeral and she said yes and went home to Seth.

Everything was just beautiful until Eileena and Endya's birthdays rolled around. Seth had baked the cake for the girls and bought dolls for them. He had done a great job and Lilah praised him for it. When he found out that Ellis was coming by with gifts for the girls he left and didn't return until late that night, missing the party he had planned. She couldn't believe his behavior! Where was the confident and thoughtful man she loved now? Did he want the kids to act as if they had gone to their dad's funeral instead of their grandfather's? They loved Seth, but they loved their father too. He seemed cool with that as long as Ellis kept his distance and didn't have anything to offer the kids. She felt bad for him, but he needed to be realistic and fair to the kids. The two relationships the kids had with them could co exist. Her family REALLY didn't like him after that. They had no sympathy for his feeling but Lilah did. She still confronted him, but she understood. Ellis went deep into drug use not long after that. Lilah knew he would not be consistent in the kid's life any way. If it wasn't for his wife, he probably wouldn't have come as much as he did. Seth and Lilah seemed untouchable, no issue ever lasted long enough to put a dent in their love. He continued traveling back and forth to California. Surprising her with romantic baths under candle light and rose petals everywhere. They were stronger than ever.

Until his boss and cousin who was also a crooked preacher. Conning folks was his hustle. Like he was some anointed miracle worker or a prophet, he drained pockets dry. Seth was his assistant, Lilah didn't like them using God's name in vain. Seth insisted he just handled the money as an accountant did. One day Seth had been running errands for "Mr. Crooked" and hadn't stopped in for lunch like he usually would. She really needed him that day because E.J. was home sick with a bad case of chicken pox. Poor kid couldn't get out of bed, feverish and covered in pox from the top of his head to the bottom of his feet. Lilah had been paging Seth all day to move a television in the room with E.J. but never got him to answer. So she finally called the ministry. His cousin answered saying Seth was real busy, he would try to track him down and call her back. She thanked him and went to check on her son. She had met this man only once before when she, Seth and the kids had dinner at his home with his family. This man was sucking on reefer like an asthmatic on an inhaler. Lilah and Seth didn't smoke so they only had wine.

He obviously hadn't forgotten Lilah or thought about her a lot because what happened next was crazy! He called back saying Seth asked him to move the television for him. He said he didn't mind mind so Lilah reluctantly accepted. When he got there, he was wearing so much cologne it burned her nostrils and eyes. Big dark man wearing bright lime green silk pants suit and matching gators. A white fedora with a black band. She thanked him for coming and lead him to the room and told him where she wanted it. When they got back to the front room he went, "Okay girl if you need anything just call. Give me a hug." with his arms stretched out for her. She was going to give him the appropriate hug that left lots of space between them, when he grabbed her with both hands at the waist and slammed her body into his. She was so startled she began pushing him off but couldn't get out of his grasp. He was too close and too strong. She was so upset at this point, with a grunt and one last push she had freed herself and was winded breathing heavily. She told him to get out of her house. He slowly turned and walked away as if she must be crazy for not wanting him. When she told Seth he acted as if he couldn't believe it. She couldn't tell if it was shock or he just didn't believe her. Seth left the house and later returned with his cousin, the man's wife. He told Lilah to tell the woman what her husband had done, so Lilah did. She had the nerve to say, "I hope you're not lying, you could be breaking up a marriage". Lilah said, "Honey, I don't think your man cares too much for your marriage." Lilah had described what he was wearing from the clothes to the loud cologne. Seth knew Lilah didn't have a car and E.J. was home sick so why would she leave and go to the ministry even if she had a ride? E.J. Himself described the man who brought the television to his room. It was the talk at the family gossip table (his) that day and probably weeks to come.

He came back home and held her all night telling her what people were saying about it. Most of them believed her. The man had a reputation as a womanizer. Something Lilah didn't even know before the incident. He first came into this family dating one sister and after being caught cheating, married the one he was cheating with. "Sounds like they are both low down to me. They deserve each other. She had the nerve to act like she cares that he came on to me knowing what he's capable of", Lilah said. Seth couldn't argue with that, but he had lost his job. She was sorry, but felt it was for the best. He moved out claiming he needed some time alone. How could he at a time like this?! What was the point of standing up for her, if he wasn't going to stand by her? He came by everyday, even stayed all night a few times. One day to her complete shock..... he was gone just like that.

He had gotten on a plane and moved back California without so much as saying a word. She was so furious when his brother finally told her a week later. Realizing he hadn't even said goodbye he hadn't even said goodbye to the one person he was claiming was the love of his life. It was surreal, then heart wrenching. She threw violent fits, started drinking and smoking reefer again to keep from thinking about it. She went on that way for a month. Her girlfriends stayed close by everyday waiting for her to cave. They knew what she had lost, they wanted to be there to console her. It looked as if it wasn't going to happen, until one day she was alone. Standing in the bathroom, to her surprise as she stood in front of a mirror, her whole body trembled. She didn't recognize herself. She was this weak frail woman who was lost. A heavy weight grew on her heart and the pain, oh the pain was unbearable! It felt like someone had reached inside and pulled her heart out and the hole that was left was hemorrhaging with pain. She ended up on the floor in the bathroom curled up in a fetal position sobbing. She felt like she was having a nervous breakdown. Lilah knew beyond a shadow of a doubt she loved this man. She had finally found love and lost it. She also realized Seth was selfish and fickle. He had called claiming to still love her and had done what he had to do for their future. That he was coming back. The damage had been done , it was too late.

Chapter Ten

She's had four major relationships, if we count Ross. The white boy between Kyle and Ellis whom Lilah had a crush on in high school. He didn't seem to notice her then but she stood out for some reason four years after high school. They had a interesting affair that lasted about as long as summer did, by Fall they had ended and badly. Pushing thirty and the pain of hard knocks, Lilah was moving on.

Having only been truly in love only once, if the brothers thought she was high maintenance before, they must've have thought she was a goddess now. No matter how mean and rigid she became, they still catered to her every whim without so much as a thank you in return. See Lilah was getting good at this this. Getting love, without getting hurt. Seeing a brother for who he truly was before she opened herself up to him. Nine times out of ten, he would have exposed himself before and any harm was done and Lilah could just set herself free again. Though there were a few, whom Lilah know she loves to this day. Warren "Snoop" Riddle , there has always and always will be a something uniquely distinctive about this brother. He never committed to her, but he never really left her either. They just had this silent rapport and adoration for each other that always pulled them back together. It never stopped him from parting and committing to someone else though. Lilah never understood why Snoop never wanted to be with her that way, but she could not shake him or forsake him. She was content with the status quo for years and finally had to decide, he isn't going to be moved.

All the women in her neighborhood either admired her or hated her. She was either labeled a "player" or a "hoe", take your pick. It didn't matter to Lilah, one thing Lilah didn't do was let people define her. In fact, she made it her business to keep them confused and stay at least one step ahead of them. If they got close to the truth, she'd create a diversion of some sort to throw them off. The world was hers and the women were just wallowing around in it in their misery, while the others cheered from the sidelines. One thing was for certain, it was one touch down after another. Another one biting the dust Lilah was kicking up in her stilettos, at a time. She was always safe, always sure. So slick, witty and full of charm, she had well earned her reputation as a "Femme Fatale." Lilah was sexy, effortlessly. This wasn't something tried to be, she just was and knew how to use it as much as she had contempt for it. She didn't want that to be the first thing you noticed about her, but it was. She just oozed of commanding and mesmerizing sexuality in a Pam Grier sort of way. More than that, her toughness was her sex appeal. Deep down, that offended Lilah, like people didn't take her seriously. Being sexy was highly over rated and being a sex symbol was the last thing she wanted. It beat being that invisible dark girl nobody noticed or loved but who wants to be noticed for the wrong reasons? Lilah was humble in heart, royal in her presence.

She'd make a good queen because she cares for people and their rights, especially women and children. Men had to earn that from her, they had to show their worth. She didn't have instant compassion for them in that regard. Unless they were elders, disabled or homeless, "They could kiss her pretty black ass", is how she put it exactly. Respect is what she commanded and she knew how to make things work in her favor. If her brain couldn't get her in a door, her sexy body and charm could. She knew sometimes you have to rearrange your priorities. Sometimes you have to put the goal before the plan. If at first you don't succeed, try again, another way. Better to get your foot in the door the wrong way and do right once you're in, than not get in at all. She was a lady about herself. She wasn't trashy with her sex appeal, she was sophisticated with it. She truly believed in the perfect blending and harmony of brains and beauty or brains and booty.

It doesn't matter what she chose because Lilah could never be labeled or defined with simplicity as simple as she was. It's because of her complexity, she's always and never the same. She's happy and sad, good and bad. She's soft at the very core of her being, but rough around the edges and tough on the surface. You have to get in pretty deep to see her softness, that's again, if you're a brother. Lilah loved the children like Jesus Christ himself and they loved her back. There is nothing she won't do for a child. The sisters, she had a soft spot for them too. See Lilah believed if sisters stuck together the way the brothers did, they'd be stronger and more effective. That they could actually force brothers to be the men they were meant to be. Her perception was this: "Men need women, they can't live without them. If women put on a strong united front and stood firm on it, men wouldn't be so out of control."

She seemed to be alone in that philosophy because sisters ran each other down over a fraction of a man while men ran them down and used them against each other and stood by their brother with that M.O.B. (Money Over Bitches) stance. Lilah is as gifted with perception of sight as she is well versed with a pen. Through experience and observation, she came to the conclusion that, "Hey, if you want to make it in a man's world you better learn to think like one". Even James Brown had enough sense to know, that even though it's a man's world, it's nothing without a woman or a girl in it. That would be the final analysis on men for Lilah, with a do or die approach. She'd tell her home girls while sipping on Hennessy and doing the ballroom hustle to the Isley Brothers "Footsteps In the Dark", " Girrrrl, you better get your shit together and rise above the big bad brother. Cause he aint gonna choose you if you always let him use you." I can tell you, they really loved and admired Lilah...... until they hated her. It's like any female relationships Lilah had could only go so far before the resentment would creep in, except the one she had with her grandmother and Natalie. Seems she was everything all of them wanted to be in some way, form or another. Lilah was a lot of things. She was like the amusement park. She had a lot to offer , main attractions and plenty of variety. The thing of it is that may have felt weird or just unreal for others , is how down to earth she is. She didn't have herself on this pedestal others put her on. So when people felt intimidated by her she just didn't get it. She was confident, but not arrogant. Life had taught her humility. Life had tried to push all of her self esteem through the mud, but she wasn't having it. She kept her feet on the ground , she wasn't laying down getting stomped anymore. Whoever couldn't deal with that while attempting to be in her life had a problem she couldn't help them with.

Life had taught her that being human meant taking the good with the bad. Winning some and losing some. The real winning is being able to accept defeat without feeling defeated in who you are as a person. She knew how to roll with the punches. More importantly, she knew how to punch back by getting up , wiping herself off and getting ready for the next round. She had been dealing with back stabbing for as long as she could remember. Most of them were women if not all of them. Let me tell you, as far as Lilah was concerned the brothers like that were women too. She had more luck with friends rather than family because the women in her family seemed to hate her the most. Yet other than Pilar, Aunt Babe was the only other person that was a thorn in Lilah's side.

Like I mentioned before, Aunt Babe had been Lilah's idol since she was a child. She was a real live movie star, beautiful and vain as hell. Eventually Lilah called her "Diva". During the time Diva had abandoned her two preteen aged children and left them with Pilar, she was partying hard and getting high, just spiraling out of control. She was a very intelligent and bright woman, another reason she was Lilah's idol. She had married during high school to an older man, her first love. By the time Diva was eighteen, she had it all. A husband, a house in a nice neighborhood, and a family. Her husband suddenly died when their son was a toddler. Lilah believes that's when everything started to unravel for the Diva. She was use to having a secure life and it was like all the walls around her came tumbling down.

For along time, Lilah had posed no threat to Diva and was one of her favorite nieces. After learning she was pregnant again, Diva vowed to get off drugs and straighten her life up. She had gotten pretty big after the birth of her youngest, two hundred and thirty pounds big! It was during this time, that Lilah had started referring to Shai, Pilar and Diva as the "Three Musketeers". They were a miserable threesome and she seemed to be the target all the time. Now everybody knows Lila was Pilar's least favorite, hell she wasn't on the favor list at all. Shai claimed Lilah just rubbed her the wrong way, she couldn't put her finger on what her problem with Lilah was. Diva would never even admit she had a problem with Lilah now. That was because she had the most ridiculous reason of all. Lilah was skinny, she had had three children and still her stomach was flat and firm without a stretch mark in sight. She wasn't sporting weave because her hair was still long and silky. Let me make a correction before we go on, Lilah was lean and mean, not skinny. She had an athletic build, great legs and a nice rear. Everything on her body was in proportion with her height. Diva use to say Lilah had the body of a tennis pro. She would say Lilah had a perfect Barbie figure and she wanted to be her size. Pilar would always say, "That's TOO little!" because her girls Shai and Diva were already perfect in her eyes. It was an insult to her that they would envy Lilah in any way.

Diva had the home court advantage, Lilah's mother and sister were already playing against her. Whenever she was under the same roof with Diva, Diva made sure she humiliated Lilah. She would put on display   ridiculous and cruel jokes about how skinny and unhealthy Lilah looked. She even went so far as to imply that Lilah was probably on crack she was so skinny. It would be years before Lilah would realize that diva was threatened by her appearance and any attention she might get that she felt belonged to her and her alone.   After all, if Lilah REALLY looked so awful, why did it bother Diva so much? It wasn't like she was being sincere or concerned for Lilah and the last thing she was, was confident. She had lost all of that weight using Lilah as her inspiration. The second she had achieved her goal, she became a mad woman with a vengeance. She acted as if it was a contest going on for the family's attention and anyone else that was around. She was and has always been the "spoiled brat who could do no wrong". It seemed everyone who was over weight enjoyed her show and others just pretended not to notice.

One day Lilah would look into Diva's eyes and swear she saw the very soul of her. It was so sad, but she realized she wasn't Diva's enemy... Diva was her own worst enemy. After so many years of asking, "Why? Why does she hate me so much when I only love and admire her? Why has she backed me in a corner leaving me no choice but to come out fighting?!" God had answered the minute Lilah decided she wasn't going to tolerate her Aunt's charades anymore. It was the defining moment she would realize she wasn't the victim, Diva was. She simply didn't know how to co-exist with Lilah.   There just simply wasn't enough room for another attractive dark skinned woman in the family, who was small and didn't have weight issues. Lilah had been enlightened and set free. She pitied Diva living in a glass house. A frightening little world where she had to be the director, producer and the star. As smart and beautiful as she was, she was too shallow for her own good. Lilah just felt if she was going to resent her that much, it should have been for something she had done to her purposely. It was something she couldn't help and certainly wasn't a crime. This woman being that selfish and mentally/emotionally unstable, that she felt it was okay to drive someone out of the family or their own mother's house so she could feel special. Delilah felt she certainly deserved to have her way because she had worked so hard for it, for more than ten years. She had the support of the family rather they joined in with her or pretended not to hear her knowing it was wrong. So that made it easy for Lilah to see them as cowards and Diva as pathetic.

Lilah didn't need the family's validation to feel special, she didn't need anyone's.

She had learned though, to trust the smiles of men and the frowns of women as a true sign that she was looking good! Nobody was ever going to make her doubt or second guess herself again. Diva had abused the respect Lilah had for her, taking for granted the love Lilah had for her and used them against her. Determined to make Lilah inferior to her. Almost ten years older and to date, still struggling to stay thin and youthful. If only she spent as much time on her heart and spirit instead of worrying about how she looked, she might not have been such a mean drunk. She is undoubtedly a more thinking and feeling person now. Perhaps her competitive streak waned with another chance at being a mother to her grandchild. Maybe she realized that all the money, designer clothes she can buy, flashy cars or weight she could shed wouldn't mean a thing when it's all said and done.

However, Lilah thanks Diva for the long and unpleasant experience. It was an unhealthy labor of love after all. See, the "Judas" of the world are a catalyst. You need a Judas in your life. Learn to embrace them without losing focus of your destiny. Lilah had three of them so she feels really blessed now. They mean to sabotage, break you down or outright destroy. Once you recognize their angle, you have to accept the responsibility to be the better man/ woman, to be stronger. The Bible saids in II Corinthians 12:9-10

"And he said unto me, "My grace is sufficient for thee, for my strength is made perfect in weakness". Most gladly will I rather glory in my infirmities, that the power of Christ may rest upon me. Therefore I take pleasure in my infirmities, in reproaches, in necessities, in persecutions, in distresses for Christ's sake: For when I am weak, I am strong." That's what God had blessed Lilah with.... Grace.

That's why no matter how "bad" people heard she was doing financially, she always looked like she had money effortlessly. She wasn't even trying to keep up appearances, she just did with God's grace! She had glorified God instead of herself for years by not confronting her Aunt. By being still and waiting for God to show her why Diva and the other Musketeers were such a thorn in her side. They all had different reason but something in common.....hating on Lilah. Reasons which would destroy no one in the end but them.

These sisters Lilah had now were thicker than than any blood she knew. She didn't know another soul that was THAT down with her except Natalie. Now Natalie is down for life, no doubt. Her girls were there for her when she had Seth and when she lost him. It was cool, because they were easier to relate to being her age and spiritual like her without being "holier than thou". Although Natalie has always been there for her like a mother and loved her dearly, she relied on her "sisters" now for comfort and companionship. That was cool with Nat, she only wanted Lilah to be happy. She wasn't stupid, she knew Lilah was living in sin. She didn't judge her and she never turned her back on her til this day. Not after that one time long ago when she listened to Pilar and Lilah ended up in a missionary shelter in a strange city. Natalie sought and received forgiveness and had proven she was sincere in her apology by never making the same mistakes twice.

Another hard lesson for Lilah was: When someone is truly sorry for an indiscretion or betrayal of trust, they won't run the risk of doing it again. If they truly value their relationship with you, they will put forth the effort not to burn you again. At least not in the same way or situation. Lilah had also gotten comfortable with the belief that nothing was forever. Be it good or bad, either way you were supposed to make the most of it. Ride it through to the next phase or chapter. Right now, she had some sisters. Sisters who relied on her wisdom and support as much as she did theirs. They respected and admired her courage, her daring personality. She appreciated the relationships she had with them and often expressed it with gifts and words. She appreciated the efforts they made to show her, her shortcomings. How impatient and detached she could be. They once got together and told her, "Lilah, when things hit a bump in our crew you don't just say fuck it! Talk it out!" Lilah was like, "Set me straight girl, set me straight" and they'd all laugh. It was their way of saying. "What we share is worth fighting FOR, not against each other." So for years to come they were there for each other. They looked after each others children, kept food on the table for one another. Went out together, threw down together, they just stuck together.

Even though her girls thought she was pretty and had it going on, Lilah thought the same of them. Dina thought Lilah was strong and down to earth. Gave her inspiration to lose weight and start dressing up and finding a career. Dina accomplished all of that and Lilah was so proud of her. She went out and bought her an outfit and earrings. She thought Dina was so cool, creative, resourceful and witty. They had a lot in common, birthdays being a day apart. When Lilah was working on a project, Dina supported her like she believed in her. They believed in each other. Dina had this electrifying smile that lit up a room and everybody in it, she was a great dancer too. Lynn was the funny one and the mediator. She didn't have the uneven temperament that Lilah and Dina shared. She was more balanced in her moods. Lynn had legs to die for! Lilah had been told she had "killer legs", but Lynn's must have been the ultimate killer cause good Lord! They all had something the other wanted, but they were amorous not envious about it.

Crossroad... to Another Crossroad
Written by De Layna Starr Brady

Before we burn bridges

We should make certain

That we do not have to travel

that route again.

For one road often leads to another

While others intersect

or lead to a dead end.

It's important to know how and when

To make a detour near the end

or stay on a road and start to recover and mend

Chapter Eleven

It wouldn't be long before a smooth operator cruised into the neighborhood. He'd had his eye on Lilah since the first time she stepped outside her apartment. Oh she saw him too, but she knew the type. First of all, he was on another woman's porch who didn't seem to like her (turns out she liked Lilah a lot and was Bi-sexual). Lilah wasn't feeling the flirtatious "Ooh you fine looking thing you" looks he was giving her from across the street and rolled her eyes at him. She walked next door to Dina's. " Do you see this "mofo" on Troy's porch? Staring all hard and shit" Lilah snarled. "Yeah he's fine too girl, maybe he's family", Dina said thinking about the time the lady across the street was trying to hook Troy up with her nephew but he couldn't stop looking at Lilah and ended up talking to her instead. "Yeah maybe, she don't seem to want him looking over here anyhow". "Yeah, and he don't seem to care what she want", Dina laughed. That was the first time she saw him.

Everyday after that he was at a different house on her block until he ended up right next door to her. Apparently, he had grew up on the block then moved to the suburbs. You could tell he had been inquiring about her and was even more intrigued by the fact that she had remained a mystery to every man in that neighborhood for over a year. She didn't seem to give a damn that this fine. Denzel Washington looking chocolate, tall, sexy brother in a classy white car was watching her like it was his business to know hers. "Lilah, that nigga wants you! He been over here everyday and no matter who he's talking to, he's looking at you", Dina said as her and Lilah was walking up the street coming from the corner store. He was in front of her neighbors' house sitting in his car, so she had to pass him. Her neighbor had been unsuccessful at getting her attention so he seemed to be warning him not to try. Lilah imagined her neighbor saying, "Yeah, that bitch don't like men. She's probably gay." They were both laughing when she got directly in front of his car but kept going. "Excuse me, can I talk to you?", he asked. "Can you get out of your car?" Lilah snapped while Dina snickered. He mumbled something as her neighbor laughed, but he got out of his car and Dina went home. He walked up to her and held his hand out to shake hers. "How are you doing, my name is Treat." "Fine, I'm Lilah." "Can I call you, take you out?" he asked. "I don't know, you can leave me a number to reach you." He asked the neighbor for a pen and they exchanged numbers. The guy on the porch next to her neighbor kept staring giving the side of Lilah's face a burn and she groaned in disgust. "What's wrong with you?" Treat asked. "I don't like when people just stare in my face", she said annoyingly. "Maybe he likes what he see", Treat replied. "Well it's rude to stare, maybe he should just say something and get it over with".

By now, Treat was probably thinking, "Man she IS a bitch!" "How old are you?' he asked her. "I'm thirty, how old are you?" Seemingly intimidated, he refused to answer. " I answered your question, you could at least answer mines" she protested. After waiting a few minutes she went, "You know what? Fine, it was nice meeting you" and started to walk away. " Hold on! I'm twenty three", he said quickly. "Was that so hard?" she asked. They talked a little while longer after that and she left to catch up with Dina. He yelled as she walked, "Call me!" "Yeah right", she thought. She had told Dina that night, "Yeah he's fine and he knows he's fine. He's use to getting what he wants WHEN he wants it. I'm going to play him off for awhile before I call him." "Go on with your bad self then", Dina encouraged Lilah.

After a week, he decided to call Lilah but she didn't answer. He kept going to Troy's house or Junior's across the street where he could see what she was doing and with whom. He was growing irritated and insulted and that tickled her. He was losing his cool trying to figure out why she hadn't called. She had met him in September but didn't call him back until January, right after the New Year. She had a million and one excuses why she hadn't called before but he was excited to hear from her. Treat was of the same mentality as Lilah. See he was appreciating her game and wasn't about to quit before it got good and he could play his hand too. For them it was, "Nothing ventured, nothing gained. Easy come, easy go and the chase is always more thrilling than the capture". She just wanted to deflate his ego a bit and redirect his interest in her to her mind and not the obvious physical attraction. Lilah knew she wanted Treat the minute she saw him. They looked good together like Billy Dee and Diana Ross, Morris Chestnut and Gabrielle Union to name a couple. Treat was the first dark skinned brother to catch Lilah's eye and hold her gaze. He was that gorgeous. Now that she had humbled him, it was time to stun him by catching him off guard. She invited him over and they got to know a little about one another. Both being pretty evasive, he cut the chase down to the real question. "So when can I get naked with you?", Treat asked bluntly. She knew it was coming because his eyes were full of lust. "The hell if I know, I haven't gotten naked with anyone in over a year. I had a really bad break up", she said. He looked like he had been hit over the head with a brick. Not only did her response put him and his mannish behavior in check, it left him dumbfounded. Next she intended to blow his mind, which was pretty much already a done deal. "What happened?" he asked sincerely. "I was engaged to this man, we were in a good place. Then suddenly he just left without even saying goodbye." she said with a sincere sadness in her voice.

They just stared in each others eyes for a few long minutes. He needed to be sure she wasn't pulling his leg and she could tell he was touched by her pain and that it was real. He had been punched in the gut unexpectedly and was uncomfortable now. He rose from the sofa to leave, "Well call me when you want to see me" he said. She stood up directly in front of him and looked him in the eyes. "If I let you make love to me, will you stick around? I don't like one night stands. I didn't preserve myself this long for that." She said it in such a way, with a vulnerability that let him know she was longing to be loved but not by just anyone. It was more than just a desire now.... it was an honor. Again, there was silence as he searched her eyes for a hidden agenda, but all he could see was how sincere and honest she was being. That he had to take her seriously, to step up to the plate or back down and walk away.

"Yeah I can do that. When are you going to call me?",

he asked. "Tonight, after I find a sitter for the kids". "I'll be waiting", he said before slipping out the door. Lilah called Dina since she was closer and told her the plan. Dina volunteered to watch the kids because she was glad Lilah was finally getting some action. She was wondering when the ice around Lilah's heart would start to melt. After the kids were gone, Lilah went to the liquor store and bought a fifth of cognac. She was so nervous that night, she was all about the house like a jitterbug. She drank a few straight shots as she contemplated on how to go about getting her groove on. She went to her room after showering and caressed herself in perfumed oil. Then slipped into a black thong that showed off her beautifully sculpted posterior and a matching strapless push up bra. She wasn't as gifted in the breast department, but she had enough to make a statement. At least they were upright and perky. "Why not give them a plunge?" she thought.

She wrapped herself up in a silk thigh-length kimono and headed back to the living room. At 11PM the phone rang, she looked at the caller ID and it was Treat. She sort of chuckled at the thought that she was supposed to call him. He must've been going stir crazy over there. "Hello?", she answered. "You ready for me to come over there? I'm across the street." Lilah knew that, she looked out the window when she answered the phone. She saw him looking out the window from Troy's house. "Damn!", Lilah thought. She realized she still wasn't relaxed. "Uh, yeah come on over", she said. When he got to her apartment, she let him in and offered him a drink. He was already holding a drink and checking her out.

He appeared to be a connoisseur of cognac and women. He sat at the same end of the sofa he had sat on earlier that day. Swirling his glass around and looking at her body from head to toe. Slowly, as if he adored every inch of her. As if

he had a detailed plan for every inch of her. He was an architect major and you could tell he knew about every structure and build. What he wanted to do with every nook and cranny to carve his very own niche into it. This made her even more nervous. She didn't feel relaxed or intoxicated at all. "Take off the robe and let me look at you", he said. Boy oh boy, was he sexy! He said that like Billy Dee said "You gonna let my arm fall off?" in "Lady Sings the Blues". Yet, he was every bit the intellectual hard care, thugged out player Denzel Washington's character Alonzo Harris was in "Training Day". The resemblance between the two was haunting!

She stood in from of him, but on the other side of the table and slowly loosened her robe belt. Then slid it off her shoulders and let it fall down around her ankles, stepping out if it. One long sexy leg at a time. "Turn around", he said with seductive eyes. His lashes were so long, they sprouted about his face like whiskers. When he spoke, there was no question who was in control. He commanded and lead effortlessly. She turned where her backside was facing him, she wondered what he was thinking. Did he like what he saw? He raised up and leaned towards the table for a closer look and said, "Girl, what have you got on?!" Lilah was kind of stunned and confused by his reaction. "Hasn't he ever seen a thong before?" She thought. "What do you mean, you don't like thongs?" He sank back into the sofa shaking his head, "You ought to be ashamed of yourself wearing that." "Why?", she was really confused now. Treat was so flabbergasted at how sexy she was, he was having a hard time making her understand that was a compliment. "Come here", he said holding a hand out for her. "Wait, I need a drink first", Lilah attempted to reach for the bottle but he was too aroused and went on the prowl after her.

He pulled her in close and caressed her body with strong, firm strokes. She moaned as her body went limp in his arms she was so relaxed as he quickly laid her on the sofa. He stood over her removing his clothing and she watched impatiently. Not that he was moving too slow, but the passion between them was intense. His body was beautiful. He tried to flip Lilah over on her belly and enter her from behind but she refused him. This is where the tables would turn again, she was in control now. She wrestled him down and he surrendered seeing it was going to be her way or no way at all. She was on top of him, she looked him right in the face and smiled before she rode him into ecstasy. They went back and forth, over taking each other for at least an hour.

It was like watching two lions wrestle for power and mate at the same time. They left each other breathless and thoroughly satisfied. It was the beginning of an adventurous and mysterious, unpredictable, tantalizing, and delicious affair. They must have counted the hours before they would devour each other whole again with unbridled passion. They put smiles on each others stubborn and detached expressions and emotions. They became the envy of the neighborhood. Very few were happy, that they were happy with each other. Every woman wanted Treat and every guy wanted Lilah. Nobody dared to reveal their jealousy, at least not before the couple would allow doubt and suspicions to creep in themselves. They welcomed the enemy by inviting him into their minds. Exposing their fears and reluctance to trust anyone with their hearts. They were both too cynical to follow their hearts and felt safer staying in their heads playing games. See that's where they ruled, the both of them.

After three wonderful months of complete paradise, they must have decided what they had was too good to be true. At least Treat did, or maybe he thought he just had her where he wanted her and could start shopping elsewhere now. Lilah may have been playing the game above his expectations now, but he had surely underestimated her. There was no doubt that Treat was feeling Lilah, possibly falling in love with her. That made him feel threatened and in a territory he wasn't in control of. He certainly didn't want to fall first or without knowing she felt the same for him. She did, but she kept him in suspense. She knew he wanted to know, but he didn't. See, they both thrived on the unknown but the need to seek the curious and mysterious. They wanted to know what you didn't want them to know because if was a form of rebellion for them. To take what you weren't willing to give them gave them power and authority over you somehow. Yet, they didn't want the obligation to love you back just because you loved them. It was like, "I need to know you love me but you don't need to know how I feel about you." He needed the chase more than the capture, who's better to understand that than Lilah?

Once after they had made love, she offered to fix him breakfast and he declined. Lilah felt that was strange, Treat was ALWAYS hungry. "What do you want then?" she asked. "I want you", he responded as if it was a lost cause to even admit it. She sensed defeat in his voice. "But you already have me", she said. "Do I?" He asked surprised with widened eyes waiting for confirmation. Lilah looked away from Treat in that moment, hesitating and stealing the brief moment of assurance she had given him away. "Yeah sure you do", she then said playfully. It would be one of the few times in years to come, that Treat would unmask himself in front of Lilah because of that. Allowing her to see his raw emotions of adoration and affections without a wall of steel in front of his heart.

The funny thing is, she instantly would regret her responses or reactions on those rare occasions he surrendered to her, but she couldn't help it. They both thrived on contradiction. Treat must have eventually decided he was better safe than sorry. After three months of acting like a man smitten, he did something unacceptable. He brought another woman on the block, Lilah's block! Right across the street from her at Troy's. Troy was loving it too. That's where the REAL games began.

The Game written by DeLayna Starr Brady

He took her for a ride, and she had a good time
Still, he got her home early. It was the romance of a life-time.

He was the perfect gentleman, opening doors...for the lady is first.
Smooth and clever he is, he knows love is her thirst.

He's the master of the game, and he can spot a winning score.
Playing all the right cards , keeps them coming for more.

He gives a generous amount, before the taking starts
The objective of the game is to play and win as a result, broken hearts.

The key to his success is physical attraction
A wink and a smile gets him instant reaction.

He's been playing so ling it feels natural
Scoring on this girl was anything but rational

She appeared delicate like a lamb, but was strong as a lion and sly as she was a fox.
She gave him just enough rope to hang himself, then blew him out of his socks.

She saved all her winning cards for last
Overwhelmed and confused, he is the outcast

What goes around will definitely come around

The shock and pain will weigh in on you, pound for
pound
SOMEBODY

ELSE

IS

ALWAYS

SMOOTHER

AND

THERE

IS

NO

MASTER

IF

YOU

THINK

YOU

ARE

THE MASTER,

IT MUST BE OF DISASTER!

Just think about it for a minute

Chapter Twelve

It was as if he subconsciously wanted to get caught, or it was time for Lilah to learn something new about Treat. She was taking a nap that afternoon on her sofa, when suddenly her instincts prompted her to get up and look out the window. When she peeked between two blinds, she saw this light-skinned, red-head with freckles get out of Treat's car and go in Troy's house behind him. She was furious and shocked, "No way is he stepping out on me. No way did he have the nerves to bring her in MY hood!" She got up and stomped over to Dina's, who was expecting her having seen the incident from her own porch. Before Dina could utter a word, Lilah had let herself in. "Girl did you see that shit?!" Lilah said pointing towards the front door. "Yeah girl, I was wondering if YOU did, who is that chick?!" Dina answered. "It aint me, that's for damn sure! You know what? I'm not going to let this nigga get the best of me yo. I'm gonna be cool for now, give him a chance to explain himself. I mean Troy's son is having a birthday party. He's already been by to see me today, so it will have to wait until' tomorrow". She reasoned. Lilah was pacing the floor thinking about how to deal with this surprise. Even Dina couldn't believe treat had been so bold, Lilah could... she had just allowed herself to get blindsided. All she had to do was think about what she would do in his shoes because she was his female counterpart. They was so much alike it was cute and dangerous at the same time. That's why she knew how to handle it. "I'm thinking there's got to be a misunderstanding, everything is not what it seems to be. Then again he could just be testing your coolness to see if he can break you in", Dina explained. "Yeah well I'm mad as hell, but he'll never know it." Lilah went home and kept herself occupied with the kids and writing poetry that day.

The next day, Jimmy gave her and the kids a ride back from the school. Jimmy was a mutual acquaintance. He knew Treat from childhood and was one of the few guys on the block Lilah associated with. He was a single father and was cool to hang with, very friendly and practical. She only liked Jimmy as a friend and had politely rejected his advances. Claiming she didn't want to jeopardize their friendship that meant so much to her. He seemed okay with that and okay with her and Treat's relationship, but Lilah always knew he was still kind of jealous. "Hey Jimmy, what does Treat's sister look like? I think I saw her yesterday", Lilah asked innocently. See when you know a man is going to go a certain route, you got to do the research and investigate in advance. You don't check BEHIND his story, you check AHEAD of it. "Oh uh, she's tall, dark-skinned and got long hair like you", Jimmy replied. Jimmy could see Lilah's nostrils start to flare and her mouth tighten.

"Why, what's up?" "Oh he had some girl with him at Troy's yesterday and I just thought she could be his sister. She doesn't fit the description though., Lilah answered. Jordan had a "busted" look on his face, "Aw shit, you done made me tell on my boy!" "No you didn't, I won't even mention you when I confront him. You had no idea what was going on." "Whoa, so you're gong to confront Treat?!" "Hell yeah!" Lilah assured Jimmy. Jimmy looked as if he felt he had to warn Treat. Lilah used her sexy, soothing tone to calm him down. "It's all good baby, let's forget about it. Come have a drink with me." Jimmy wasn't too bright, getting one over on him wasn't hard. Especially if he thought he was getting closer to Lilah. He was the type that would mess around with her behind Treat's back but throw her under a bus if Treat found out and leave her with the responsibility of the whole betrayal.

He liked her, but he respected Treat's game. Treat did for the fellows what Lilah did for the chicks, played the players game with skill. Jimmy went home all buttered up in sweet talk and no sugar, to be exact... in Lilah's bullshit. On time and on schedule, lo and behold walked in Treat. Lilah was so cool and laid back, she even greeted him with the same "Baby it's good to see you" smile she always gave him. It was obvious Jimmy hadn't warned Treat. He was his charming self, not suspecting a thing. "How could he not? How could he bring somebody over here knowing that I myself or somebody I know might see him?", she thought quietly. While they were talking and all cuddled up, she asked him "Who was that girl getting out of your car yesterday baby?" he was definitely surprised. "Uh, oh that was my Sister", he said with a nervous laugh. "No it wasn't , your sister is dark like you. This skinny bitch was high yellow with red hair", Lilah said as a matter of fact. "Oh HER! That was somebody in Troy's family I picked up for her. I brought some people to the party that didn't have a way. How do you know what my sister looks like?"

Treat was so caught that even if he intended to start

this fire, he was worried about getting burnt himself now. "A little birdie told me", Lilah answered in a low and disgusted voice. "Jimmy's big ass mouth told you didn't he?!" he asked, half angry and half smiling. "Nope, whoever it was didn't mean any harm.

Was just saying something not knowing what it meant to me", Lilah said. "Well that wasn't nobody baby, trust me. It was no one." "Okay baby, if you say so. Let's just put it behind us", Lilah said cool than ice in a freezer. "You don't believe me do you?" "I said let's drop it didn't I? I am satisfied with your answers, are you?" Lilah manipulated. "Yeah, yeah let's drop it." Lilah laid her head down on his chest and they fell asleep together until it was time for him to go to work. She fixed him a lunch and kissed him good bye.

Dina couldn't wait for him to pull off so she could ask what went down. "Girl, give me the dirt and who's the dirtiest!" "Girl, he lied right to my face... he played the sister card", Lilah said disgusted. "No he didn't?!", Dina said just as disgusted. "Then when that didn't fly, he said he didn't know who she was. He was playing taxi for Troy!" Lilah was so insulted. She was out for blood. Lilah never turned down a challenge. She was being challenged in a way that was so tempting, it gave her an adrenaline rush. "That's a pitiful ass excuse girl. What you gonna do? I know your ass is cooking up some special shit for him", said Dina. "You know me so well, and you know it's got to be special cause Treat is special." " Oh Lord! I'm scared to know what that means now. Listen Lilah, I know you're mad but maybe he realizes you are not a fool and that was bad judgment. I don't think he's going to be doing it again", Dina reasoned. "He's still seeing her though. Of course he won't be so impulsive again, but he has somebody else and I don't", Lilah argued. "So, you gonna two time him back?" "No, but I can make it look like I am. Give him a taste of his own medicine. He needs to be reminded, I'm still anybodies game too", Lilah declared. "Ooh I like it, but it's risky. They don't like when we start sassing their asses." "That's where I'm different from most women Dina, I don't give a fuck!" "Oh Kay! I got that", Dina said, feeling chastised. " I mean seriously, I've been looking at this nigga through rose colored glasses. I still want him, but I can't afford to get boring and predictable. It's obvious the nigga is comfortable and feels he has me. So he can take some of our time and spend it on new conquests. He's got to feel me slipping through his fingers, you got to keep their asses working or get worked!" Lilah explained. "I feel you so what's up?" Dina asked excitedly. "Do the bees work for the honey?" "Yep" "It's time to make him work, he's already sweating... enough said", Lilah concluded. Lilah and her girls went out that night. The kids were with their dads.

The next day at the school, Lilah saw an opportunity. This tall light-skinned brother she had briefly dated winked at her. He was so full of shit and weak ass game, Lilah just wanted to kick his ass every time she saw him for not having no game. He was trying to talk to her and some desperate ass female at the same time. Talk about variety! Lilah could care less, she was just sexing him at the time, and that wasn't great. It must have been to this chick, because she was always giving Lilah these "Get your ass back" looks and guarding him like he was her property when ever Lilah and her girls were around. They would burst in laughter on her silly ass every time, making her even madder. So Lilah asked him one day, "Damn baby what's up with your girl?" "That aint my girl, we are just friends. She got an older man, we cool that's all", he said. "Okay cause um, she be getting real ill." "Aw it aint nothing there baby, you got to have faith in me girl" Lilah looked him up and down and rolled her eyes with a scoff in disgust. "Nigga, I could have all the faith in the world in you, and that wouldn't help your sorry ass okay?"

He was so intimidated by Lilah that he instigated some shit between this chick and her. He had the girl thinking her life was threatened Lilah wanted him so bad. When Lilah heard the chick was coming for her, she decided to save her the trip and come to her. Her and her girls were ready for whatever. First and foremost, she wanted Anton to be there because her beef was with his corny ass. She wasn't the type to fight over a man. She believed, "If a brother was for YOU, you wouldn't have to." She called him the night before and told him it was time to walk like a man. He showed up begging and pleading, trying to explain how things got out of hand. Lilah cursed him out so bad, humiliating him in front of everyone. That chick didn't want none of that. She started stuttering and proclaiming she had a man.

"Good for you sister girl.... you don't know me!" Lilah said. "Y'all need to get your shit together cause aint no man up in here", looking at Anton. Then pushing him aside and walking out. Nobody said a thing until they were two blocks away.

"That bitch know the old man aint hitting it. That's why she's sweating his weird ass so tough", Lynn laughed. "You know?!" Lilah agreed. After that,every time he saw Lilah, he would charge pass real fast like he had a stick up his behind with his nose in the air. Wasn't for long though. He started speaking again and eventually called Lilah and apologized to her..... "Whip cracks"! He had told her her toughness made her even sexier. She had been cutting brothers with her mouth for years. Truly, she would cut them with a blade if they didn't get the message fast enough. After their swollen egos had been deflated and pride was healed, they had to respect her for who she was.... bout it! So there he was, tortured and tamed. Lilah saw an opportunity and she took it. She could teach two "motherfuckers a lesson with one plan", she thought.

Chapter Thirteen

"How you doing dark and Lovely", he asked. "I'm fine baby how are you?" "Pretty good, what you been up to?" "Nothing much, you?" "Thinking about you", he answered. "Here we go again", Lilah thought. "Oh really? Well why don't you pick up some take out and bring it by my place and tell me all about it". She suggested. He was so happy she invited him over he offered to take her home too, which was exactly what she wanted. Jimmy saw her leaving with Anton and called for her. She told Anton to get in the car, she'd only be a minute. Since she had rode up there with Jimmy, she felt she owed him an explanation sincere or not. "What's up man?!" she asked. "Hey where you going girl? Jimmy asked concerned. "Oh I got to get something before I head home and Anton offered to take me", she lied. "You think that's a good idea?" Jimmy asked as if he was trying to warn her. "It's not a bad one, I'm not doing anything wrong. I'll catch up with you later." "Okay Lilah", Jimmy said disappointed.

She had Anton buy her two orders claiming she was that hungry. One was actually for Treat. She knew he was going to flip out and she needed to calm him and have an alliance at the same time. She had no intentions on inviting Anton inside. As soon as they got on her block, Treat was coming up the street. She tried to keep her cool, it was too late to half step now.

Somehow she knew she had gone too far. She had to finish what she started though. She was feeling a lot of things at the moment. Fear, courage, conviction and guilt. So far everything was going according to plan. Just as she suspected, Jimmy had called Treat and told him Lilah had left with someone else.... a man. Lilah knew he would, he felt guilty for telling her about Treat's sister, He felt he owed Treat one. The look on Treat's face when he drove by her in Anton's car was chilling, but he pulled in Troy's drive way. Lilah's heart began pounding as she watched him get out through the side mirror and storm in Troy's house. Anton could tell something was up because Lilah hadn't said a word in the last ten minutes or so. A few minutes later, her pager started going off. Before she could read it, it was going off again! Treat paged her about eight times and the vibrations from the pager sent tremors through her body. It was as if he was telling her, "You better get your ass out of that car bitch!" "Is everything okay?" Anton asked after seeing her look at her pager constantly. "Damn I'm sorry, no it isn't. Something has come up. Listen let me take care of it and get back to you in an hour?" "You can't even eat your food first?!" Anton said realizing he was being sent off. "Like I said, sorry. It seems to be urgent and private", she said getting out of the car and watching him pull off. She pretended to be just as disappointed as he was.

As soon as he was gone, she headed across the street to Troy's. She rang the bell like four times before he came down. When he did come down, he acted like it wasn't even him blowing her pager up like a mad man. He was all cool and relaxed. "What's going on, is every thing alright? I mean you paged me to death while I was sitting right there in front of my house", pointing at her driveway with an innocent and concerned look. He looked at her like, "Yeah right" and said, "I'll be over there in a minute." She said okay and went home. He was pissed but kept it concealed good like she had done days before. When he got there she was eating the take out and acting her usual self the way he had done. Before he could say anything she said, "Here baby I brought you some food, you hungry?" "Yeah thanks and who was that nigga?" he asked. "Oh that was my brother", she said snickering. "Oh Okay! So it's like that?!" he was truly pissed now.

She started laughing and teasing him while he pushed her away. "NO seriously, that wasn't nobody. He works at the school and I asked him to take me to the carry out to get us some food. I didn't feel like cooking today." "So Jimmy couldn't take you?", he interrogated. "You know Jimmy's car can't make it out the hood without falling apart and getting dehydrated", she laughed. "You full of shit nigga", he snarled. "Why are you so mad?! Okay dig, I used the situation to show you how it felt when you said that was your Sister but I aint trying to talk to that nigga. I got us some food and that's all I was trying to do, okay?" He stubbornly nodded in agreement. "Here baby eat your food, I was just playing when I said that. It was a joke. If you were telling the truth the other day, you shouldn't be mad, right?" she said. "You're right, fuck it let's eat." He ate, they talked and made love, then he went to work. Clearly, she had him messed up, he didn't know what to do with himself. He played it off, but he got sucker punched!

Lilah and Dina hooked up the next morning over coffee and bagels. "Girl that is your best play yet!" Dina said. "Yeah, and truly I hope it's my last. I want to be down with Treat, but he's got to respect me as his equal", Lilah explained. Treat was just like Lilah though, it was about getting that last word or laugh for them. She knew deep down, it was just the beginning of some trials. That even though he started it, he had to finish it too. Lilah just wanted to even the score and move on, she wasn't calling the shots though. Treat wasn't about to be dominated by any woman, no matter how bad he had it for her. He was truly hurt because she out-smarted him and turned the tables on him. She could do that in the bedroom, but that was where he drew the line. It was only one way he could see redeeming his reputation and that was to dismiss her.

That day, Treat didn't show up so Lilah paged him. He called her right back sounding like he was still in bed. "What's up?", he said. "Are you okay baby?" He sounded depressed to her. "Yeah, I'm alright. I'll see you tomorrow." "Okay, bye", Lilah replied. She could tell she had really gotten to him. "Let him sulk, he'll be alright", she thought. Two more days went by, so she called him again. He had officially broken pattern with her. He called her right back again, this time he sounded as if his confidence had been restored, "Hey , what's up?". "You, that's what's up. What you getting into?" Lilah asked. " Listen, I don't think we should see each other again", he said. Shocked out of her mind, Lilah asked "Are you sure that's what you want Treat? Cause I won't be calling you again" she said hoping he didn't mean it. He didn't, but he was about last words right now. "Yep I'm sure."

She was so hurt, you could hear it in her voice like you could hear it in his days earlier. "Alright Treat, good bye." "Bye!" It was in that instance when they were disconnected by a dial tone, that she realized she loved the man more than she loved the game. He had made her feel inferior in order to restore his superiority. She found herself dazed and confused in the next week. Her girls teased her with jokes like, "Girl, you done met your match, ha ha!" They weren't ever lying either. She knew this meant he had met his too then. A match is a match you dig? She simply had to be strong and go on about her business until he realized the truth of it. You don't know you can love a person until they can keep up with you. They had to have the endurance and "balls" to get ahead of you. Every time you push them back, they'll keep finding their way if not beside you, in front of you. From the beginning, Lilah refused to walk behind Treat. He was a player. Everything he did personified who and what he was. When he was with a woman, he walked in front of her and let her follow. Not Lilah, she made it clear if he wasn't going to walk with her he could look at HER backside and watch HER ass switch away from him. Treat had to decide he could appreciate a woman that made him work but rewarded him with love, loyalty and great sex. She had to have his respect though, love doesn't last without respect. To him, showing her he respected her was like admitting to defeat. She was a woman for God's sake! A week later he started showing up on the block again. Chatting with everybody except her, he knew that would burn her. He wouldn't even look at her, at times he'd burn rubber pass her on the streets to show his resentment. "Girl, you know you got him good don't you? Be strong, that nigga is doing all of that because you got under his skin real deep and he tried to play you", Dina assured Lilah. " I know man, but I don't wanna play no more!" (Music to Joe's "I Don't Wanna Be a Player No more")

Lilah was buckling under pressure, but her girls kept her going. "Lilah, that's exactly what he wants you to do. He wants to regain control. If you surrender now, he won't get the challenge you can give him", Lynn coached. Here her girls were giving back the lessons she had taught them. They were paying it forward. They thought she was too blinded by love to think for herself right now. See ladies this why sisterhood is so important. Lilah wasn't blind though, she was about to teach them something else. She simply didn't care about winning the game now, she wanted to win the man.....the prize. "Sometimes you gotta give in, it's not always about winning an argument, but the bottom line. Treat doesn't get that yet. Me letting him win shows I'm still on top of my game. He may think he had broken me in, but the point is to get back in. Once I get back in, eventually he'll drop his guard again. By that time, I will have fucked him into oblivion, got into him so deep, that he won't be able to live without me", Lilah said staring into space. Dina and Lynn looked at each other spooked. "Damn, this bitch is crazy aint she? She don't quit!", Lynn said. "You're damn right I don't and neither does Treat. We're in it to win it", Lilah replied. "You motherfuckers are like Ike and Tina. Taking turns beating each other down with macks!" Lynn joked.

That's how it was the first few years, back and forth. One things for sure, they were inseparable.... even when they separated. They came to understand that there was nobody who could deal or thrill them like they did each other. They got so real with each other, respected each other's game so much that one day Treat said, "You know what? Fuck it, you fucking niggas and I'm fucking bitches. There it is! It don't change shit cause nothing can come between us. Sometimes we just need to do our own thing cause it keeps us balanced. I'm ALWAYS going to come back to you cause you're always there for me without drama and judgment."

Everybody knew what they had was strong. She let him be who he was and he did the same for her. Seven years later, she gave him a party for his birthday, where he was the recipient of a threesome. Only there were three women instead of two. She had to be pretty secure in their relationship to pull it off, and she did so superbly. He had been trying to get her to do something like this since the first year. Lilah knew there were other women. Like I said he wasn't hiding it. She had even done some of their hair. It was another one of his ways at testing her. To see just how strong and stable she was emotionally. She passed every time. Hell he was paying her to do their hair. Then what ever plans he had with them went to hell cause he would drop them off and come straight back to her and they'd end up humping like rabbits. This is the type of amusement two players need to keep their love alive and kicking.

She watched him sex those girls on his birthday while she sipped on Hennessey. After they had watched him make love to her first, of course. He was so blown away by her coolness, it scared him. The next morning he told her, "You're a very bad girl, but you're MY girl." "Always" she responded. Everybody knew Lilah was Treat's Queen by now, even Lilah. Like most things in life, once you achieved a certain level, things aren't what you hoped they would be. Treat was losing equilibrium, he couldn't separate the streets from home. The "hoes" from love, he was in a dark place and didn't seem to care how he treated Lilah sometimes. She suspected he might be on drugs cause she barely recognized him at times. Lilah was growing tired of his impulsive and cruel behavior. He was always dual, but he had split into a "Jekyll/Hyde" role that was too much for her.

He would force himself on her when she refused him. Break in if she didn't let him in and even threatened to kill her a few times. Lilah's words were coming back to haunt her, "He won't be able to live without me, I'll be under his skin so deep." He had made it clear to her, "It aint over til it's over!" It was like she had put some type of spell on him even she didn't know how to break. Everyone, especially the elders who had known Treat since he was a boy were like, "Girl, you done did something to that boy. You can't leave him but one way now, through death." That scared Lilah. She loved this man, she didn't want to leave him, but she didn't like the thought that she COULDN'T if she wanted to. Not because she was afraid to or addicted to his love like she once was.

By this time in the relationship, all of her girls were gone. They had started hating on her over the years, all she had was Treat and her children. She became depressed, didn't get out of bed for a week except to send the kids to school. She seriously considered escaping him through death, but she couldn't abandon her kids like that. She made a phone call to the one person in her life Treat didn't know... Natalie. He couldn't find her there and she knew it. She never talked about Natalie with him. He only knew she was like a mother but nothing else. He left for work one morning, and Lilah packed up the kids and left. Jimmy saw her loading up a truck, she was afraid he would contact Treat before she could get out. At that point, even Jimmy knew the relationship had taken a fatal turn. She made it out, but she was still weary and grieving. She always thought her and Treat was the one constant in her life... the one forever. It was like she knew it wasn't going anywhere from where it was but down. They had gotten as far up as they were going to get and it still wasn't what Lilah wanted. She knew Treat could do better , he just wouldn't. If he wasn't going to try anymore, neither was she. He wanted her to take him for what he was, which she did. She just couldn't cut herself down trying to love him anymore.

She went back once to retrieve some things while he was at work. Not that he ever lived with her, but he just owned the neighborhood. She always felt if she was going to be in it after things went bad, he was going to have to be out of it and that was only when he was at work. He had stabbed up the sofa and ransacked the place pretty bad. Her and her sister got chills up their spine and hurried out. She knew she couldn't go back to him, she had kids to think about. Eventually, when she moved into another house of her own from Natalie's. She did reach out to him again. She still loved him for a long time after that, but it was over. Treat eventually let go and accepted it. To the point he didn't even want to see her or talk to her. It was like, "If she don't want to be down with me no more I don't want no parts of her." That hurt Lilah, she really wanted to stay in his life but he refused her at every attempt she made. She conceded with the perception maybe he was finally doing the right thing by her. He set her free.

Chapter Fourteen

All Lilah ever wanted was to be able to love without losing herself or her lover, seems she could never have both at the same time. She wants someone who can love her unconditionally without judgment. Who can appreciate her flaws as much as her qualities. Someone who understands that she has bore all things on her slender shoulders. That she can keep up and stand the test of times. Although Treat accepted Lilah, he still didn't trust her with his heart completely. To her, she had given him plenty of time to know he was in good hands. She only has so much time to waste on anybody and she gave him more than she ever gave anybody. She has learned with time and age that game can cripple a man mentally and emotionally. He has to be winning all the time, the one who survives and actually wins will be the one who surrenders. All the great players are only for a season, they played long and hard and they were like Gods. Yet, they knew when to surrender or retire.... and they are still great players because of it. They played to win, now they're playing to live. True players have a quiet confidence, knowing they have proven themselves.... to themselves. Letting others struggle to compete, keep up and follow their leads. So now when we consider ALL things, the things each individual has had to face we realize judgment is a delicacy. No one is above the law that only God can judge, because only God is perfect. When we play the "game" of life with respect for God's law and love for us. With respect and love for ourselves, we cannot lose. We may crash, but we will not burn, sink but not drown. So there is hope at every ending, chapter and phase. So there will always be pain, sorrow and lost, it's how we comprehend these things. How perceive and conduct ourselves regarding them.

We wonder how even the strong can be weak and vice versa. Well I'll tell you what I've learned through the course of study and growing up with Delilah. That even when we are weak, we are made strong through Christ. Being Christ-like requires some weakness in order to glorify God. It's called humility. For when God is glorified blessings abound. Delilah was born humble. When her innocence was stolen, she was lowered to yet even more humility. She may have even hated herself but she was a dreamer and hopeful. In her adolescence, God had already begun to orchestrate in her life. He was beginning to show her that the pain in her life was just cause for the joy in her life. That she was always favored for her meekness. That sometimes others fear that there is something so great, and so special about a person. Fear that somehow they might pale in comparison to or be over shadowed by another. Envy and resentment are ugly siblings born of misery. Misery is born of hate and insecurity.

When God brought Kary into Lilah's life, he spoke volumes through him. Saying, "You are beautiful and worthy. Nothing they have done to make you feel inferior to them matters now. I will show them where they cursed you they have instead blessed you." Even the blessed has to stay on guard and alert against evil.... evil is always looking for a way in. For a way to cheat you out of your happiness. So even though God and Kary found Lilah worthy, the resentment and contempt those close to her felt overrode their opinion of her and the one she had of herself. She was under the impression still, that THEIR opinions were the ones that counted the most. Let it be established here, that Lilah had very low self esteem even though she was tough as diamonds. Toughness was an exterior defense to protect her interior offenses. A person who believes they are worthless will run everything good out of their lives if he doesn't destroy it first. She was once told by her step dad that she "Looked like a movie star but wasn't shit." Yes, by the same man who spent her childhood calling her ugly! Then acknowledging her beauty was only blossoming with age, giving her credit while deducing her at the same time. Tormented and enraged, she knew not rather to prove him wrong or accept his judgment and self destruct. She chose the latter, until she found God. God further and divinely worked in her life and on it. Through Pastor Kilborn, his wife and Natalie. They managed to reach her in a place only Kary and Grandma had been. Delilah needed more than just a tap on the heart. She needed a deep, penetrating, soothing and enlightening kind of edification. The Holy Ghost provided such an experience and taught her forgiveness was healing power.

It wasn't long that Lilah discovered that although she was vulnerable, she was resilient. She had been "bouncing back" from something all her life. This is where she began to realize that everything that happened in her past was instrumental in her future and her purpose. She kept God in her thoughts, but he wasn't always in her actions. Which is why she found herself fluctuating between good and bad relationships. Always, all in all, Lilah could find fault with herself. She could learn from her mistakes. If her pride didn't get in the way, she was ready to start over, better equipped. Pride and egotism are foolish traits or characteristics. They steal your ability to be humble. When one is without humility, he is susceptible to idiotic behavior. She would make round after round of foolish choices. I believe because she was able to laugh at herself during these times, God remained merciful giving her grace to be sufficient.

Sometimes she skated so close to the edge of a situation, she was bound to meet the point of no return. Sometimes the point is NOT to return, but turn a new leaf. She took risk not many dared to take, escaped wraths only courage could break. What I admire most about her is, she could say things like, " There are things and people I really loved and God took them away from me or me away from them. I respect that even if I don't fully understand or fully appreciate it because he knows better than I do, what's best for me and what isn't. He knows when I can't do what needs to be done, so he does it for me", and smiles in awe of her savior. Delilah knows who her best friend is just like she knows she felt she needed a man's touch. She also learned not at any cost is a man's touch necessary. Not of it gets between you and God. You need God to get that man, find that man and keep that man. More importantly, to get YOUR man who was made for you. Delilah can say, " I've had as many men love me as I've had lust me, but none of them truly belonged to me. He's still out there somewhere because of my foolishness, his or both." By the time G-Money arrived on the scene, Lilah had given up so much. What she gained was well worth the sacrifices. She was whole, alone but whole. The only love in her life had been God for some time and it was enough. She didn't have as much money, material things and arrogance as she boast in the past, but she was so much richer. She had divorced a family she felt was only getting "sicker" , causing her skin to get thicker where they were concerned. She had finally come to understand they weren't necessary for her survival or success. That they were either helping or hurting her cause which made her decision inevitable because they were almost always not sincere. She was thankful for a lot of things, she realized them being who they were made her who she is.

Sometimes a person's cruelty can set us on a good journey, in the right direction. Somewhere they themselves need to explore but too righteous and stubborn to go. Some are just too cowardly. She definitely knew she was brave. She'd tell you embarrassing things about herself with no shame, to her it was liberation because, "Everything you go through and get through is your testimony to others. Not just the outcome, but the income. The price you paid for the outcome. New students cannot benefit from half a lesson. How much you're willing to give can change the outcome of what you can get back. I once told a troubled girl the story of my life. Where she didn't have hope before, suddenly she did. She couldn't believe I was so bold and would expose certain things that people hide all the time. It's because they find it hard to believe that somebody understands and can relate. That somebody can listen without judgment and speak with compassion.

Courage breeds courage, If I dare, someone else will dare" Lilah said.

Lilah knew she was meant to be instrumental in how people saw themselves, but she first had to see herself realistically. The blind cannot lead the blind. She was content where she was and whom she was. She certainly had come far. She certainly appreciated the small and simple things. She was finally buying a home even if she was one year shy of forty. She had raised three fine children by herself. She's touched a lot of lives with love, respect and honesty. She had come to a place in her own heart where not just women and children were special, but men too. She had a respect for all humanity alike. She was free in a way she'd never been. She knew how to love an agape love now, without expectation. Wide open, withholding nothing. I'd be willing to bet my life, this is what God wants in all people. Loving without fear of losing. When you love whole-heartedly and lose, it's only temporary. You'll soon find it was their lost, not yours. This does not mean we should stay in bad relationships subjecting ourselves to pain and unhappiness. You're supposed to have enough sense, spiritual insight to avoid "those" altogether. If you should have a slow awakening, make a speedy departure. Better late than never.

Chapter Fifteen

Two weeks after she broke it off with G-Money, he returned. He had been humbled by her courage to walk away and not settle for being a "friend with benefits". After several attempts of sweet talks and negotiations that worked to no avail, he was giving in to the power of love. Lilah had hoped for such a revelation, but remained skeptical and cautious. Once it was clear to her that he was surrendering to her demands for her love, she too surrendered. To her dismay, the same night they would celebrate their committed union, G-Money was arrested for possession of narcotics. She wasn't just hurt because they were blown apart as soon as they found their way back to each other. She knew there was no good that could come of the life he had chosen. He had argued with her many times, "NO, you mean no good could come of the LOVE we share in the life I've chosen. There's no room for love in this lifestyle!" So he tried to choose money first and Lilah later.

He told her it wasn't forever, but just until he had a foundation to build from. He was a good person with good intentions, but lacked good judgment. "There were so many men who deserved to be locked up more than G-Money", Lilah thought. A crime is a crime, wrong is wrong. For days she played the same song over and over, "Time and Chance" by Color Me Badd. The lyrics, "Good man's down while a bad man's standing tall, strong man don't always win them all", made her break down into the rage of pain and tears she tried to repress. Here she was alone again. Before the final tear could dry and stain her face, Lilah realized God had done his thing again in her life. Truth be told, eventually, G-Money would have dragged Lilah into his world and out of the secure place she had finally positioned herself in.

A man can only play by a woman's standards for so long. He'll make you believe it's your turn to do things his way. Whatever way you choose or boundaries you set... stick with it. If he chooses your way, then he should be able to live with it and vice versa. After all, he's the man and he's supposed to be able to lead. We need to be willing to have patience. Patience to find the one whose standards and values are the same as ours. For every Adam there's an Eve. Delilah and G-Money had a lot in common, just not on the same level! The fact that he wasn't ready to settle down when they met, proves it. He had no business "shopping if he wasn't buying". She was always going to advance ahead of him because she always did from the beginning. He'd either try to keep up or fall behind, but rarely would they be on the same page in accordance and harmony. He had out-smarted himself into thinking he could manipulate life and love. He was pulling his biggest con on himself, because God wasn't having it. Now he was sitting up in jail wondering why he chose the things he did. Why he was so hell-bent on living so destructively. Funny thing is, he was coming around and changing his mind but it was just too little too late.

Lilah had cleared away every leaf with every lesson life has taught her. "Thank you Lord", she said as she let out a big sigh of relief. "I know you didn't save me from the entire heart breaking situation, but you saved me from the worst of it that was yet to come. I'm sure glad I have you to look after me and my welfare."

Delilah had already been crowned Queen, by God. She'll be alone until she finds her King, also crowned by God. They'll know each other right away by the regalia each gracefully displays. He won't be struggling to keep up or get ahead of her, but by her side effortlessly. He'll have the same quiet confidence. Don't be afraid to stand alone, try to be home when love comes knocking, God needs you to be in the RIGHT place, not at the club with "FeFe and them". He shouldn't have to hunt you down. Though he has the power to reach down into the earth and put each person in the arms of "the one" he doesn't. Life is about learning, discovering and searching. It's about joy and pain, living and dying. The longer it takes for us to stop moving in the wrong direction, the longer it'll take for destiny to take place in our lives....leaving love lost in translation.

God does offer direction and instruction, but we need to be spiritually in tune and eager to obey him and not our flesh. While in the arms of the wrong person (wrong because you're just in it for sexual consolation), love has missed you once again. You've waited so long to find Love, that you can't tell you've found his lazy cousin Lust instead. His purpose is pleasure, limited at that. Many times lust has abandoned you because you expected characteristics from him he does not possess. He was never as bold and brave as love. He is NOT Love, is he Lust. You cannot expect Love from Lust and Lust from Love. He can only please you to a point, then he goes back to origin and starts all over again. Love knows not where it ends or where it begins really. Pleasure and happiness are two different things. Lilah has had both, and now she won't settle for one without the other. Yet, she finds both in her life every day with the people God has given her to love now. Her children, nieces, nephews, and grandchildren. Elders and strangers. She knows in the midst of misguided pleasure, you can still feel real low. Your hearts being neglected while your body's affected.

So no matter how much she may enjoy Love's cousin lust, she's smart enough to recognize him by his actions. She's smart enough to trade cousin for cousin's value. In other words, "You aint getting what you aint giving." Lust won't be reaping all Love's rewards here. We give too much for too little. It's okay to give what's yours to give if you want to give it. We must come to understand our bodies belong to God until someone Buys the rights to them from God with his approval. If that's just not your thing, or beliefs, hey who am I to judge you? Just know that whatever your beliefs, they should serve you well. Just be good to yourself. Make sure you're not being used and abused and constantly coming up short. If you know he's not the one for you and just passing through, stay clear about it when he's "jumping on another train". Don't get lost or caught up thinking you can turn Lust into Love... it is what it is. Don't let it come it come down to him "laying the pipe" real good, breaking your heart and spending all your money.

When brothers started asking Lilah for money, no matter how sprung she thought she was, she disappeared on them without hesitation. It was like,

"Hey, I'll play the fool for so long, but that's all folks". She's too tough, too cool and in full bloom. She's a wildflower! Every one of us is a flower with or without the wild. The wild is the growing, the experiences. When all of your petals start to stretch out above you and around you. Your crown is glowing standing out in the center surrounded by your growth and wisdom. You can hold your ground where the wind blows harshly. You may get pushed around and knocked over in violent storms, but the sun will come and it's warmth will pick you up and revive you again. Aiming to please an admirer passing by, who will choose you from a field to be his. Take you home and care for you. Embrace the very essence of you. The aroma of you and your uniqueness, the way your third petal curls up where another's is stubborn and stiff.

You have to become the right person to receive the right person. You've got to go through all of your baggage and find the kryptonite in your life that's weighing you down and release it. Some baggage is good but travel light nonetheless. You'll find we carry other people's baggage around. You'll say, "Hey this aint even mines, what is THIS doing in here?!" Some of it is blame others left us stuck with to deny their own shame or guilt. This is burden, leave it behind. Then there's constructive , instrumental baggage that we keep to guide us and reminds us where we've been. They are pointers for lessons and experiences we will reward someone else with along the way. I would strongly advise you to carry a bible. The best tool you'll ever use. It fixes everything! The best therapy you'll ever get comes from Jesus, and it's free!

Carry that bible literally in your purse or pocket. Keep the word close at hand. Carry it in your mind and be well versed in the scriptures. You can count on designated ones to pop up when you need them. We have got to be willing to let God move things in our lives in order to change the socioeconomics of our lives. You have to go all the way back to find the root of the strongholds. Sometimes it's good to go back, necessary to go back before you can go forward in good faith that you're heading in the right direction. There is a reason that you were eager to love and expected it to be automatically reciprocated. Those of us who grew up in a loving environment and was a recipient have been exposed to the positive early on. There is a reason somebody else may doubt love is out there or feel they have to settle for less. Those of us who grew up in a dysfunctional environment and was a recipient of such have been exposed to negative early on.

You can come from nothing and no where

And become everything and everywhere

Be ever powerful in knowing you are

Somebody special.

Chapter Sixteen

Then there's the favoritism, goes all the way back before Christ. Delilah and Pilar are the Bible's Jesse and David. You see the very son Jesse didn't favor is the very son God called to be King. God calls all of his children to be something of significance. However, greater is he that was thought the less of! I'm not saying that to say that (although it is written, it is also circumstantial) favored children are cursed. That would be a biased mentality. Jacob and Joseph are biblical evidence of this. Joseph was Jacob's favorite, it was Joseph's arrogance that hindered him, not his father's favor. Sometimes favor spoils a child and cripples a child against himself. He becomes handicapped because of favor and codependent. Unable to relate without it. Needing humility and reformation. Even though Joseph's brothers were jealous of him and sold him into slavery, he needed to be humbled. He was always rubbing his favor in their faces and he expected favor everywhere he went which was a misconception. He was daddy's Prince and somebody else's slave.

God allowed Joseph to suffer in order to teach him he had to love being ordinary in order to be special. He was a good kid though, Like Lilah's sister Shai. Favor can cripple a child mentally and emotionally when he realize the rest of the world doesn't see him through his parent's eyes, and outside the realm of his parent's influence. He has to PROVE himself worthy to everyone else. This can be a psychological blow and the confidence that was once firmly in tact can begin to slowly or rapidly slide off it's hinges. Example: A lover who could very well be jealous and intimidated that her life displayed more love than his. Being that he's jealous, he will work to strip her of her self esteem. Suddenly, the person who once thought he/she was a prince/princess is a pauper at the feet and mercy of his oppressor. You can tell who the "Mama's/Daddy's girls/boys" are too. They're raised to be weak because they have been too sheltered. Life will either strengthen them after a few rude awakenings, or eat them alive. Like Joseph, they have to have a will in their hearts to accept humility without defeat. Although he was spoiled, he wasn't rotten. He didn't allow being spoiled to undermine his role as a man, and he had a kind heart. God could use him once he recognized his gift was to enable others and not himself. Delilah could see Joseph's quality in her sister Shai growing up. As a child, Shai was generous and compassionate in her nature. The problem was, she was raised to believe she took precedence over everybody else. While Lilah was raised to assume the opposite was true for her. In Shai's adolescent years she struggled between generosity and selfishness without fully acknowledging it. Believing she was being generous when she was actually being selfish. This kept her from giving all she was capable of giving in a single deed.

Yet Lilah maintains that of her immediate family, it was her sister who kept her going and gave her hope. She was always aware of the shifting and dual face of Shai, but Shai's love proved to be the most genuine most of the time. She was simply a people pleaser and all over the place. She didn't believe in "biting the hand that fed her", even it the hand was "dirty". She might admit it to you, but not them which made her appear cowardly.   Like all people, she had her faults, but she's not a bad person. Which is why Lilah could sympathize with the pain and heartache her sister suffered at the hands of an ungrateful brother. No matter what her sister was raised to think she was (a Queen, a Princess), in the end... she is. Not because her mother favors her, but because God does.

Her expectations for herself were high and made low, while Lilah's were low and made high. No matter how different we are in nature and how we were raised, all women need to bring their expectations and standards up while being humbled in spirit. Now let's get real about the sisters who think they're doing better or rank higher based on things their men buy them. Who are always talking about what a brother doesn't have. There are some good men out there ladies. Some practical, hardworking men who love and respect women.   Too many of us have twisted the concept of what a good man is. The size of his account and material possessions don't make him a good man, it just makes him a more sought after man. In fact, a man will hide behind those things, the compensation for which he is sorely lacking in character. Especially if we're talking a bout a brother who doesn't have an education and working a corporate job. Then there are brothers not very well educated but working and thriving for better things.

They'll work two jobs if they have to. He may not have a lot of spending money after he has paid the bills, but he owes no one. He keeps food on the table and shoes on the kids feet and his woman warm and happy. If he can't drive her where she's going, he'll walk her or ride the bus with her to make sure she's safe. He helps out with things around the house and has time for you. He's probably "Good Times" James Evans, but with time , patience and love he can be "The Cosby Shows" Cliff Huxtable or George Jefferson moving on up. Never assume a brother is nothing or nobody, that's how you ended up with that womanizing knucklehead who's about nothing, especially you. He validates himself with worth based on his "dirty" money and "bling" and of course, the fact that he can buy and lease women.

I hear people laughing and gossiping about couples who live humbly. Their relationship is based on some real solid though, love. They're laughing at them too, the way her man has her jumping through hoops for the security he himself doesn't have a concrete patent on. I'm not saying you have to be poor and raggedy to be happy and have a good man, I'm saying if you got to be poor and raggedy for a while so what! The important thing is being happy and having a good man who going through whatever right there with you. Even more determined to please you because you are there for him while he's struggling. He'll find a way to the top being fueled by love and support of a good woman. Some of us are such beggars and choosers, you can't be both. Ironically enough, the ones that think they're choosing are the beggars!

Circus freaks doing tricks and acts for rent money , car notes and gifts. Is that hoop feeling like it's starting to get too high for you to jump through? Guess what, it's going to get even higher. That's why I say get right to receive right. Take care of yourself. If "Mr. Right" shows up, you'll actually be able to enjoy him... broke or not. "Mr. Right Now" Is hindering your progress and personal growth. Mr. Right won't let you do anything for him that strips away from his character and dignity as a man. Whatever you all do, it will be on his budget not yours. If you want to pitch in for extras on the date, he might be cool with that. "You want extra butter on your popcorn? Sure, go right ahead." I'm telling you, a "Manly Man" is no joke! You got to recognize him when you find, he's King. He already more than likely, thought highly of you the day he asked you out.

Be real clear, just because a brother has kept a sister "blinging" and provides her with a glamorous lifestyle, doesn't mean he values HER. It simply means he's paying the cost to be the boss. The money is obviously a form of power for him to manipulate her with. A good man (rich or poor) will lead effortlessly in confidence of who he is and doesn't need to use money to keep his woman in check. She may look like a Princess but inside she knows she's a pauper, pleading and selling her soul for the security he offers. The More money/power he has, the more women like her he can afford. We have got to learn to be strong and whole within ourselves in order for a man to respect and understand our value and virtues.

Example: G-Money offered up a pair of expensive, large gold earrings to Lilah. A "peace offering" because he had vainly made the mistake of thinking he could down play her. He put a physical flaw of hers on display and admitted it was something he couldn't see himself dealing with long term. She made it clear she was disappointed, but felt it was his lost. He too was flawed. She said, " You had better look at a woman's strengths and weigh them against her flaws next time fool. I don't feel any less confident about myself, only about you!" So when she turned the earrings down telling him she couldn't be bought, he was even more subdued. She couldn't take a gift from a man she didn't feel respected her or understood who she was. What she had lost or what she had gained from it. So if her being deaf in one ear made him uneasy, he was free to go!

She could see by accepting it, he still wouldn't take her convictions seriously. They were beautiful but flashy earrings. Tempting and tacky at the same time, like some women you feel me? She would know when he was sincere. There are differences between guilt and sincerity, pity and honor. Later on, his gifts were not only sincere, but befitting of her character. They didn't have to be extravagant, just meaningful. Men and women alike have to learn to respect each other as equals. We can't demand respect without change and we can only change ourselves. The way we think, feel and respond to the world around us. We can get better results in the same relationships presently available to us with new attitudes. In other words, the most stubborn and arrogant kind can change once he's met someone who commands his respect and won't give in to his superior attitude. Someone who's been subdued by his manipulations for years can turn the tables if she's serious about a change.

The thing of it is, she has to have a secret account and a place to stay, just in case. I don't know why women don't think about using these "investments" wisely. Why she's so lazy that she just wants to "sit pretty" and be catered to knowing damn well it's just a matter of time before she don't look as pretty or young and will be replaced. If that's what a man is about, a trophy. You can bet he's a collector and one is never going to be enough. Like I showed you earlier with Lilah and Treat, some brothers just have to have the last word or final say. He may not even consider that you're right or that you're worth it. When it looks like you got him working, he may just decide you're too much work and split. Never fret though , because too much work usually means he's lazy and wants something for nothing. Which is why he was willing to pay/buy as long as he doesn't have to invest emotionally.

Go find a real man honey, one that will not only work but put in over-time. I once heard a respectable preacher man say, " If a man can conquer himself, he can conquer anything else." That is true no matter how you might interpret it. My first interpretation of this quote came from my own experience with being self-destructive. For me it meant, if one can defeat himself or accept defeat he's already better at it than any enemy or foe could ever be. If you can keep yourself down, or in bondage. You can surely do the same to anything or one who loves you. A later and more positive interpretation came with wisdom and maturity. That is, if you can overcome personal iniquities that get between you and a better you, you can overcome anything.

The first thing we always have to deal with is ourselves. If you can't manage yourself, how do you expect to be able to manage anything else? God doesn't want us to blow our inheritance. Therefore, he keeps it from us until we are ready, responsible and mature enough to be trusted with it. If our inheritance simply and only included money, he probably wouldn't mind us blowing it. Money has no value to God, people however do. We inherit people who have been ordained to us. In an attempt to protect, God can withhold.

Chapter Seventeen

To protect us from ourselves by denying us our inheritance prematurely. It's like deciding to put a spoiled child through a series of life altering situations before blessing him, to ensure he appreciates and understands the value of the blessing. So God protects our inheritance, guaranteeing a reward at the end of our Struggles. Take joy in knowing that somewhere out there is your happiness complete. To even begin to fathom that, you have already understood that happiness is found inside yourself first. You have to have it in order to maintain it and attract it to your life. Apply it first and the rest will follow. I've found that I can persuade the most stubborn and disagreeable person by mere example of what I was trying to sell them. The reason I knew I could do this is because the example had been set before me. It made me want to experience another persons joy and peace. I saw it as brave for having taking a chance on a negative spirit such as mines. I also noticed that, whether I was impressed or not, the person would not have been affected by ME! They would have continued on their merry way and I said right then and there, "I want some of that!"

This is something Delilah has learned to do in her life presently. Be on her way and be merry. Not carrying things around with her she knew wouldn't be helpful in her journey. She doesn't mind picking up things and people along the way, she understands that is part of the plan. The point and test is to know which ones to pick up. To pick up the ones who share your vision or who don't quite have one but trying to find it. Those who only need a boost or aid for a broken wing and had to wait for someone else to walk that road and rescue them. They want to continue to soar on their own, you won't have to carry them far. We worry about that and other things too much and miss out on doing something great for ourselves while helping others. That's what really matters in this life.

Delilah once took care of a sparrow until it could fly again. When it did, it didn't matter to her that she couldn't tell if he was grateful or if he'd remember her. It only mattered that he COULD fly away and that she HELPED him achieve that. There was a time when she would have dwelled on being used. That there were folks out there (male and females) who took from her and her life and never looked back when they had the strength to stand on their own. It hurt her sometimes and sometimes it didn't bother her at all. Now it never does because she understands now what she didn't before. We set people free the way God sets us free. If you don't expect anything from a wounded animal but for it to get well from your care, that's all you should expect from your fellow man. Love flourishes in free will of itself in us.

The reason we mourn what we've lost is because we haven't learned to have peace with what we've found. We haven't learned to have peace with the bad experiences as well as the good. Until we do, Lord help us! Help us before, during and after. Let us give glory and praise to God, in all things having faith. It is surviving the bad things that make us triumphant and victorious. When we can line our adversaries up and store them in a curio and smile at them as if they were fine collectibles. Hoping for more to add to our collections. They are our trophies, proof we have accomplished some things with success. Getting closer and closer to our inheritance. More importantly, being made ready and worthy of it. I heard a man say, "Thank God I didn't meet my wife when I was still full of shit!" He knows how blessed he is now. He knows the blessing would not have been recognized as such if he was still blind and ignorant.

He's enabled himself through growth to appreciate and enjoy his inheritance. God kept this person from him until he had done some work on and within himself. I'm sure she needed to do the same before God would allow an intersection for them. Your mate is flawed too. But somehow, your strengths compliment each others weaknesses. If you are complimenting a person who does nothing but make you look bad, there's no balance or equivalence in the relationship. That's why I say we must respect each other as equals. This starts in your relationships with your parents, goes into the ones with your peers and then your spouses. Equivalence is a necessary and key component to the potential and success of all our relationships. I'm not saying children should run over there parents as their equals, I'm saying parents should respect children as people with feelings too and vice versa. I'm not saying, wives should run over their husbands and make him feel incapable running things. I'm saying husbands should respect their wives as equals with feelings and ideas too and vice versa.

Just because one person failed to see our value and worth doesn't mean we should stop valuing ourselves It means just the opposite, it means we should fight just as hard to prove we ARE worth our salt. That God didn't waste a grain when he created us. It means getting stronger after every frog you kissed before you find your Prince. It means not giving up and say, "I'm tired, the next frog will just have to do." By doing so will mean our Adam will never find his Eve. Boaz will never intersect with Ruth. Too often, a woman who has been through hell will just assume she's supposed to be miserable and unfortunate until hell catches up with her again. Wrong! We just need to be more like Ruth. Don't think about your own problems or yourself so much. Help somebody else and be happy about it. Take care of somebody else problems if you can't fix your own. That's how it works, God will fix yours through somebody else just like he's fixing somebody else problems through you. You never know, the answer to yours could be connected to theirs somehow.

Boaz found more value in a humble woman than one of his caliber. Where she was weak, he was strong. Where she was poor he was rich, and you had better believe he was weak and poor in some way that she compensated him. He had a need for her just as much as she did for him. God can orchestrate things in such a wonderful way at such a crucial time. You won't be able to help but acknowledge only God could have done it. Nothing is impossible with God. If you feel you've waited a long time, maybe you should be doing something while you're waiting. It makes sense to me that none of us is so ready we can just sit around and wait. I don't mean we should put on a tight, short dress and go to the bar or even church and look either. If we need to look anywhere it's the mirror, the mirrors of our souls. This will keep us busy enough Once we've dared to look inside ourselves, and face things about ourselves we know need improving... there is hope. I will be the first to admit, I'm still working on me. It will be a work of art, a master piece in the making. Some will say , "What the hell is it?" looking sideways and others will say, "I get it". While someone will say, "That was made just for me!" I'm still finding too much gray and black here and white in areas that need vibrant colors there. Still finding weeds and pulling them out. For every weed I've uprooted, I've planted a seed of hoping a wildflower will manifest. Proof we don't have time to sit around feeling sorry for ourselves. We can instead choose to fix ourselves. Part of this restoration is reaching out to others. Being selfish is a dangerous thing. If Ruth was too busy trying to find a new husband to care for her, she might have left as soon as Naomi told her to. Naomi said, "You are no longer obliged. Look out for yourself." Ruth couldn't leave the old woman, it just wasn't in her character. She insisted she was not going to leave the old woman hanging. She stood by her and made sure she ate everyday. She put herself in a position to be discovered not even knowing it!

You don't know who's watching you when you're not looking. Let God watch for you, cause God knows just what to look for. He's got complete coverage and able to stay on top of things. You know how much faith that gives me? More than my mind can begin to grasp or wrap itself around. In the mean time, I'm taking care of business and my family. Investing in my inheritance so that it will be even more than God himself intended. Now if that don't say "I know I deserve the best", I don't know what does! God's already given us incentives, rebirth, grace, understanding, family, home, health and a vision and a promise. He's shown me how to use my gift to help others.

It's like when a parent has a heirloom/ inheritance he wants to pass on to a child. He's excited about giving it to the child so he'll give you as much as you're willing to grow to handle it. A mother may have a platinum and diamond watch her mother gave her she wants to past down to her daughter. At first, her wrist was too small, then her maturity and sense of responsibility was too little. She's only going to give what she knows you're capable and ready to handle, but she's anxious. So is God. You think you're tired of waiting? God has been at the finish line waiting on many of us to get there yesteryear! He also appreciates the fact that some of us is more focused on pleasing him on our way there. He knows when we intend to bring all we can to the finish line. Believing in our hearts, we have made ourselves over inside and out. We don't have to be one hundred percent made over. Truth is, we may never be. Enough so that God knows we are ready to intersect with "the one". God knows part of the reason two people are made for each other is because they help groom each other into being their best. Who is better for us than God then? NO ONE! The person who can finish your thoughts and your sentences, knows how you feel and what you want without a word being said. The two of you are one of a kind. We've given up hope. We keep telling ourselves this is too much to ask for. Why? We lack two major ingredients in our mental make- up.

1)Belief that God loves us
2)Faith to have great expectations.
If God is greater than all men, created all men (in his image), certainly he can "design" us one. If God loves us, certainly he wants what's best for us. We say we want the same for ourselves, but our lives and our choices say different. One of the hardest virtues I've ever had to learn is patience. I never cared too much for the truth and consequences as I did action. The mistakes and consequences almost seemed worth the trouble as long as I was never bored and was doing something even if I was repetitively falling down and getting back up. Isn't that how a baby learns to walk?

Chapter Eighteen

The kid must've fallen on his behind a hundred times before making it to one piece of furniture to the next. The whole time, someone laughed while they watched closely to make sure he couldn't really hurt himself. That's what God is doing, from time to time he picks you back up. He gives us room to fall, but his hand is always shielding us. He's proud that you're determined and bold enough to keep at something until you get it. That you want to grow and become independent. God never wants you to stop growing or striving. Our whole lives is about growing and learning. As much as it seems a task, it can be done with joy. I've slowed down a lot. Some people call that mellowing. I still live for the action, but I stop to smell the roses now. Slowing down has given me the benefit of enjoying the ride and the view that comes with it. There was a time when my mind raced in my head like a train of thoughts and everything went by like a blur. I didn't actually, taste, feel nor smell any of it. I discovered the wisdom to acknowledge I may be passing something greater than what I was actually reaching for.

There are things and people all around you ,you've never noticed before. Taking the time to "smell the roses", is more than a figure of speech, it 's one of life's truest and surest joys. Having this attitude when approaching everything you do can give off refreshing optimism. God loves the small and simple, he makes them bigger than life! He wants us to savor the small things before graduating on to bigger things. It represents the pattern of life and growth. Small things turn into big things. Why is it we want so much when we've shown appreciation for so little? Ignored the little things that held significance, for something bigger yet superficial? God knows when your values and the value for everything in your life is in proper perspective. He knows just how much to trust you with and when to trust you with it. Many times, we've had a house full of things, but no house. Meaning if we don't have a stable foundation to house those things, it won't be able to hold them or us. Sand castles crumble and wash up on the shore leaving little or no evidence of it's existence. We long for solidity but fail to endure the patience it takes to build from concrete decisions. Brick by brick, we've got to reconstruct our housing(spiritual house), to make sure we don't fall apart. The decorum may not say a lot. It may not be anything to boast about, but at least your house will be on solid ground right?

We can decorate it later. When I do, it won't be to please anyone but God. Whatever God gives me, I'll give it back to him. For He was always the owner. If we are willing to return the things we cherish back over to God, we show we cherish him more. He let's us "hold" things for awhile, love things and people for a time. Your father won't mind your husband so much, once he realizes he can never take his place in your heart. So it is with God. He will give you to someone who loves you as he does, with pleasure. For the time being, love with a smile to a stranger. A kind word. Help someone, get to know God and his plan for you. Believe me, his plan is better than YOURS. If yours worked , you wouldn't still be looking. If yours worked, you wouldn't be divorced. If yours worked, you wouldn't have such bitter memories to swallow. What have you got to lose , when you consider what you've already lost... by trusting God? How much more is your plan going to cost you?

Delilah has taught me many things. One of my most valuable lessons has been this, no matter how bad some things hurt you, it could have always been worse. You're still here because God isn't done with you and what didn't kill you just made you stronger. You've heard that a lot and you're going to keep hearing it until you get it. God is still molding and shaping your life. Delilah has said, "Pain is so normal, so essential and habitual, that life just isn't complete without it. If I lived a period too long without pain, I would have to inflict it upon myself by pinch or slap just to make sure I was still here, and not yet in heaven." She's saying we're going to hurt all the way to heaven where it stops, but God's going to love us all the way through it. He's going to give us strength as we give him glory. Show us favor and teach us to walk with grace.

When Boaz comes through on his chariot he'll say, "Who is this woman?" Her strength and frailty will exude such a graceful beauty, everything around her will pale in comparison. She has chosen the hard road, the road less traveled. She has chosen to fall behind in order to help someone else. Risked being mocked and ridiculed by humility. Yet there is something special about her. God has given her beauty for ashes. Fine stones of amber, ivory and onyx for grains of sand. The house that once burned to the ground, that collapsed in the gush of a wave or slipped through the fingers like fine grains of sand has been resurrected. Boaz saw something in that field that was unique and alluring. He owned the land, but what made that land significant was not his. He knew Ruth made everything he already had seem common.

THIS is what we want ladies. We don't want to make an impression that will only have a temporary effect. That merely put a dent on a man's mind. We want to be THE answer to his prayers! Something substantial that impacts our future standing. What we didn't know was God's "man" is led to us through him. God was watching Ruth, and led Boaz to find Ruth. This is a repetitious process that goes down in history. I insist, God's plan is better than ours! I can't tell you as of yet, that my own life is proof of a happy ending. That I've found my Boaz or my Adam, the end has not yet come for me. I'm on this journey right along with you. I am optimistic that time is on my side. That my happy ending is nearer rather than farther or at least looks more promising. I'm in no rush, I've learned to enjoy every little thing as it comes. To be content with what God puts in my life NOW. Maybe you thought the next thing God put in your life would be a man to love you, but instead he gave you a grandchild, or a friend. Someone needing a home. Just do it and love it.

My spiritual growth is my reasoning. I am a servant of the Lord. I am a servant first and a recipient last. God has placed people in my life currently because I can help them in some way. When you feel you're losing something that was vital to your well being and reason for living. God knows how to fill the void before it empties. Before my own children could move out on their own good, the same number of children was put in their place for me to love. I had so missed the tender years when children are young and depend on you. So missed the days when my love and affection and concern were not embarrassing and annoying. When a child needs a kiss and a hug and likes being held. Teaching, raising and protecting children is one of life's most rewarding and joyous tasks. It's one of the things that make me feel whole. I'd be lying if I said there were days I didn't feel I could do it anymore. Days when it took so much out of me, I'd thought I would die or go crazy without a time-out. God gave me grace and occasionally a time-out. During those time-outs, I found myself longing and anxious to reunite with the children. Now that they're older, I wish I didn't take any time out at all. It all goes by so fast, but the younger years are the most vital and precious. Children, it is my forte and I know this now. My life will be spent surrounded by children rather there is a Boaz or not. My Boaz, will have to be someone who wants to help children and people in general. That will see how our time together will be enriched by serving together. There will never be enough children and sisters for me to reach out to. It helps me to help others. To show God's love for them through myself.

I may be just giving something else wings to fly away from me. You know what? I don't care, I'm glad to know there are more broken wings healed because of me and the God I serve. I know that no good I ever did, no love I ever gave had an impact without God's hand in it. Which means any losses I felt, God felt them too. God has watched many of us fly off in another direction without him. Whether we return to him or not, he loves us and wants us to be happy. He's hopeful we'll realize we still need him even though we are strong an independent. No matter how good things are going for us. He wants to hear from us when we're happy too. He wants us to lift that wing that was once broken in praise, honor and glory of him.

Chapter Nineteen

You've got to be willing to be a friend before being a girlfriend. A helping hand rather than having your hand out. I assure you, in due time you'll reap what you've sown. God is watching and moving his man one square at a time. Just as single mothers expect anyone who's interested in them to see their kids as a part of the package, so do fathers. Some of these men will be single fathers ladies. We shouldn't have to divide our time between a love and our kids. They should show an interest in bringing things together if they are serious. I once had a friend I couldn't see much because of his obligation to his family. I simply wanted to be included in his interests, therefore I became interested and invested in HIS because naturally I care about children too. It's a slow process in which each person takes little tiny steps towards one another. Trust has to be established before love is acknowledged. Patience is all important in bringing all things to fruition. Fools rush in, but the wise are slow and steady.

I still felt the invisible shield this man held between us, but I also heard the silent plea for understanding. To understand why he felt he had do this alone. Why he felt it was too soon to bring someone else into him and his children's lives. He was determined to handle his situation without the support of women outside of his family. To prove he is a man and a good father. Bravo baby ,bravo! You get mad props from me. Just remember one thing, that's the main reason God wants to bless you! A person who doesn't beg or whine and handles his business like he expects it to be hard is blessed as much as he is a blessing. God wants to ADD riches to your life. Having a mate partner who shares and supports your goals and concerns is a rich addition. He may also have a hard time opening his heart up again. Once he realizes you are doing all you're doing because it makes you feel good, he'll open the door a little more at a time.

I have learned it is better to love than be loved, and not have loved at all. Why? If you've never showed anybody love, what right do you have to it? Love is so precious it should be shared and spread around. No one should ever have to live without it. Passed on from one touch or smile to the next. Being the recipient is good yes, but being the giver is great! Everything good that God has blessed you with (even if it was just a joke that cracked your side), should compel you to share it with your fellow man. That's what's so special about children. They appreciate the efforts and the gifts more than we do. Their faces just light up, they don't even think about letting pride or embarrassment get in the way of their joy.

Once you've gotten to a place of giving and serving as a priority, you won't be overly concerned to get a receipt because you're not looking for a refund or exchange. Give without expectation of getting something back. When a heart and it's motives is that pure, God will make sure that you get something back anyway! Love may not have the face or name you thought it would. Come from where you thought it should, but the bottom line is … it has arrived and on time! Your search will be over when you have stopped looking, start living. Do things that count and that put you on the map. Living in dying places take us off the map. God's map of moving his men strategically and methodically to the right place. Remember, living is living for others and ourselves but enjoying it along the way. When your life energizes and generates another life. Resuscitating a life that's lost hope and the will to go on. Helping someone find joy in their struggle by sharing it with them.

Carry their cross with them the way Simon did with Jesus. Often times and like Jesus, it wasn't even their cross to bear, but they did. "My sister aint too heavy", is a good attitude to have especially if she's trying to carry herself. Most of the time, she's carrying a group by herself, she could use and deserves some help. God is showing us we carry the cross Jesus died on by bearing the cross with others.

That's right carry yourself right on over to God's favor and grace in your life. Walking in the direction where you see a need rather than turning your back and going the other way. "Some of you are thinking, "I've done this, I've reached out to people! I've given plenty and still I'm alone and have nothing to show for it". First of all, you have something to show for it. You just don't value that in which you have gained as opposed to what you EXPECTED to gain from it. It's far more important and valuable. You have built up character and put yourself on the map. You've caught GOD'S eye. Unfortunately, you were more concerned with catching a man's eye. When you didn't meet with your expectations, you withdrew your kindness from the world. That light that was meant to shine in your direction started to dim and move away from you, putting you in the dark.

We retaliate against God and the world not understanding he works systematically. He was teaching you to build up on character and deeds that would prepare you for the harvest you invested yourself in. He's saying, "If you can get my attention, you can get anyone's attention". God's "man" is alerted through him, so be unconditional in your giving. The day you decide to hold back or give ultimatums could be YOUR day. When we revert, God's system is shut down and thrown off. God's man could have been a block away, heading towards you and suddenly couldn't remember why he was headed in your direction! Have you ever seen this? I have! Someone coming towards me with a smile and then suddenly look puzzled and turn around. I reach in my purse and get my mirror out to see if I had food stuck in my teeth... and nothing! Often times they will say they thought you were someone else. Maybe he did, or maybe you were supposed to be someone else. I digress, he turns away and he too is lost in translation.

The thing I never gave thought and consideration to is the possibility that God's man has been ready for me, but I kept shutting the system down and causing a setback in God's plan. I don't know about the man for me, whoever he is, but I have reverted from my mission and calling many times. That's enough to make me cry when I think about how I've hurt myself. It also makes me stronger and more determined to stay on course now. It teaches me that no matter how much time I may spend on a thing or person, I could be giving up just when something wonderful is about to happen. It has opened my eyes to the realization something good comes from everything I put into from the start.   Growth , character, peace and joy. You have to have these things when you get there. So when it's done, rather it ended the way you wanted it to or not, you leave with what you came with and some more knowledge. You're not lessened by anything unless you choose to be, you are extended. Who wants to meet up with you if you don't have these outstanding qualities? Nobody but the devil. Think about all the joy you've brought others, it's never for nothing and certainly shouldn't be in vain.

When we get up, it's usually because we were down first right? So falling down or back is means for getting up, a baby knows that much. Lilah use to say, "I'm already down, aint no where for me to go but up!" and "If you back me in a corner, I'm coming out fighting!" That's the spirit in every retrospect! When the going gets tough, the tough gets tougher! There are people who won't get up, won't fight back, they just take everything lying down with shoe prints all over them...literally. Everything and everybody has passed them by. They think they're only hurting themselves so it doesn't matter if they've given up. What about God? What about Boaz or Adam? You gave up and didn't follow through on your mission he'll never find you. God's heart will break because he thinks the world of you and wants you to get back in the race, but he loves you regardless. Your man out there is always going to have this hole he can't fill. A space he just can't complete because no one else fits just right, the way you would have.

There will be two souls wandering opposite sides of the world longing for each other. Imagine yourself in a maze, and you know someone else is there with you. You just can't seem to find each other. If only you don't quit, you're bound to find one another. You've got to keep going and keep making everyday count, all the while focusing on anything but. You've got to be able to tell when you're making progress or going backwards in life too. Remember how much ground you've covered already in order to see what lies ahead of you. Leave something on that path that is you. Like Hansel and Gretel left the bread crumbs so they wouldn't get lost. Of course they were eaten. Leave something inedible, that will look back for you if you return. Like a happy friend you made along the way, saying, "Honey you need something, you lost? I remember when you came through here and what you did for me."

Doubt and confusion gets in the way of success. Who better than the devil under a guise of a friendship, to get you to doubt yourself? To get you to doubt yourself when you're in full flow? We should remind ourselves when we've been good to others. WE should remind ourselves when we've been good to others. When things are good and life is smiling on us, then we suddenly get a notion that we're making a mistake or fools of ourselves. We should remind ourselves that's it's about time and keep reaching for that brass ring! God didn't bring us out this far to take us back again. He brought us out to bring us into the promised land! There is a designated promise for each of us. All I can say is, I'm having a good time figuring things out for myself, one day at a time. Be easy now, don't be stressed about a thing. Like I said, you got to take time to enjoy the small things first. They are really extraordinary. I'm thankful for the opportunity to revise my perceptions , making me even more enterprising where I was once shamefully lethargic.

There is a lesson and perhaps a message, in everything we do. Perhaps we missed too many a clue regarding "you know who". Yet I know if I stay on course, the next chapter will hold a more promising glimpse into the future. I know I'll see the answers more clearly and understand the directions better when I hear or feel them. I'm not waiting on "Boaz" to be happy and enjoy life, I AM happy and enjoying life. I'll be doing that when he recognizes me.

Chapter Twenty

I challenge my sisters to keep their heads up and dare to be a woman who's determined to meet God where you are. God has always been within your reach, but all your senses have not been within his. You have to open your eyes, ears and heart to him. He then opens the world up to you. The things that were of no avail to you before, will suddenly be at your disposal. Now don't go disposing of things you've waited for a long time before you are sure you never really needed them. Sometimes that's the case. I personally, through experience can tell you that God is faithful. He hasn't failed me in any other area I sought him, so I know he's not biased to love. God IS love. He simply wants us to understand love in it's purity, but not try to understand love itself. We spend too much time trying to understand why love is the way it is, instead of just trying to love and enjoy it. When we understand love's purpose, we have a better respect for it's power and presence.

The free gift you were born to receive is God's love and if you knew this with your whole heart you would be so complete. You'd have no fear of loving without expectations. You'd want to share that joy with the world. God is slowly changing the images the world had taught us to have, to the ones he meant for us to have. Today Delilah and I are one and the same, integrated into a healthy and whole person. She is who I use to be, but very proud to have been. If not for her, I would not exist. I can look back at

Delilah with joy to remind myself how far I've come. I'm thankful for the struggles and shortcomings, for they have given me strengths and advantages. It has been both painful and glorious, to watch myself be born through Delilah. Yet knowing I come from such a tough and determined source, a fighter and a true warrior with the heart of a saint gives me instant hope and victory. Nothing life throws at me can ever take that victory, I get that now thanks to Delilah. She saved herself by passing the ball (rebirth) to me. That's what a team does, in order to win we must work together. You've got to integrate the your mind, your heart and your soul into one mighty force. If you want to win , you've got to beat all the obstacles and the weak areas they can't get in. If you are strong in the Lord and within yourself, nothing can stop you.

Lilah understood that parts if us have to die in order for greater parts of us to live and prosper. She lived the hardest part of our life in order for me to see the blessings that would come of it. Life will still be hard and get tricky, but she has equipped me for battle and triumph. What I'm saying has nothing to do with your parents, it's all you and God. The person you were born as may not have the courage and love to grow like the person you can be reborn as does. Who you were was only meant to get you to who you will be. Change is a natural part of life. Change for the better is a challenge in life. You look at this story now and you see two characters instead of one. Lilah and me, the author and narrator. To show the distinction between the two as past and present, but one whole person. We will always be together and one. For she lives silently in the corner of my memories to enjoy the fruit of our labor.

The way Moses watched his people enter the promise land knowing his purpose had been fulfilled. After Moses led his people to freedom, Joshua led them into the promise land. Do you think the rewards for Moses were any lesser in value that he could not go all the way? No, his reward was greater! He allowed God to use him to carry out that plan, he got to see the one he passed the ball to take it home and if that's not enough for you, He went home to be with God! He retreated to heaven where all he does now is chill. The work is ours now, and we're best not to let them down you feel me?

Get the person you've grown into, in a position to carry the ball (your life) to the position that liberates you. That promotes and completes you. You're reinventing yourself without being any less true to yourself and your purpose. Every good thing I do, every obstacle I conquer is all in memory and love for Lilah. Who are you and who are you meant to be? Your name doesn't have to change, but your characteristics and objective for your future will change your identity internally and eternally. I was ready to take the ball the day I was born. I was ready to remunerate on behalf of Delilah's and my reconditioning. She gave me the key to survival: the Bible. She taught me to never let anything in life separate me from it. She read to me and fed me, she coached me and let me see where I could right her wrongs. It's what keeps me together in this life, prepares me in this life and rescues me from this life. The bible is my auto-pilot that navigates me to do the will God allows me to be his co-pilot in. My focus is on the things that I exist to improve and make changes for in the betterment of me and others. The growth, education and self-esteem of young women foremost in my heart.

Delilah left nothing to be inquired when she spoke of her trials and tribulations. Her loves and her losses. She leaves much to be desired through me. When young women discover there is life after pain. She strives to set an example for her own daughters. Encouraging them to love with wisdom and leave when you have to with courage. Become whole and independent. Stand out, be your best self and for God. I will leave my legacy to my children to carry on through generations. "Never walk in anyone's shadow", she declared. Delilah stepped down in contentment, trusting God with the rest. When she was able to do that, things changed. She saw great things happen. Pilar would even be transforming, Diva would find herself so busy doing something that put her on the map, she didn't have time to worry about the superficial things and how small Lilah looked.

It is out of great and profound love, that I pass the key on to my sisters(young and old) and mothers. I care so much for you and your happiness, that I release my passion onto the pages in this book. In hopes that my prayers are answered for you. That you have not just been entertained, but find yourself enterprising through divine intervention. I'd die a little more in order for you to live. Most of your being reborn will come from your willingness to die a little to who you are now. It doesn't mean you are a bad or unworthy person, we were born worthy. It just means we are an unfinished, unpolished and incomplete person. You were and always will be worthy and loved.

Take the key and open up your future today, step out of the past and into the present because the future is not that far away. Get yourself a bible, wipe the dust off if you have one and use it. Apply it to your everyday life, the answers you seek are in there. The bible is you GPS. The most valuable assets you possess have not been activated in your life, your bible. Many of us own one, but don't read or use it. It's funny we know when we need to go to the tool box and grab a hammer but not when to grab the bible. The last thing you need is for the past position to creep back into the present one and sabotage the future position. That's why God is so essential, because we presently get vulnerable and discouraged into withdrawals. Causing the past to try and come back and compensate in am area he isn't qualified, putting the future further behind than necessary. I challenge you to put God's plan to work in your life. Wherever you are, whatever stage of life you're in. You're bound to see significant changes starting with your foundation. A firm and stable foundation keeps us from slipping, sliding and sinking. The "ship may rock, but it won't sink with good anchorage". I'll let the power of the scripture do the rest! God Bless You.

The End

Wildflower Lyrics written by Dave Richardson

She's faced the hardest times,
You could imagine
And many times,
Her eyes fought back the tears
And when her youthful world,
Was about to fall in
Each time her slender shoulders,
Bore the weight of all her fears
And a sorrow no one hears
Still rings in midnight silence
In her ears

Let her cry,
For she's a lady
Let her dream
For she's a child
Let the rain,
Fall down upon her

She's a free and gentle flower
Growing wild

And if by chance,
I should hold her
Let me hold her for a time
But if allowed just one possession
I would pick her from the garden,
To be mine

Ummmm....................
Be careful how you touch her,
For she'll awaken
And sleep's the only freedom,
That she knows
And when you walk into her eyes,
You won't believe
The way she's always payin'
For a debt she never owes
And a silent wind still blows
That only she can hear
And so, she goes

Let her cry,
For she's a lady
Let her dream,
For she's a child
Let the rain
Fall down upon her
She's a free and gentle flower
Growing wild

Let her cry,
For she's a lady
Let her dream,
For she's a child

Let the rain
Fall down upon her
She's a free and gentle flower
Growing wild

She's a flower
Growing wild

She's free.......

The   Departing   Gift

My Prayer for my sisters around the world.

Heavenly Father I pray,
That you will touch their very souls and teach them
to be free. Free as you have helped me become
during the process of writing this book. Teach them
that running way from self and their story is not
freedom, but facing self and their story is freedom
and the beginning of new life. The unfolding
evolution of that life. That you will give them
beauty for ashes, joy for pain and understanding for
chaos. I pray for wisdom and grace to whispered
into their hearts like a summer's breeze, but strong
enough to make a resonant roar that will not be
denied.
Thank you Father, in the name of Jesus.
Amen,
Love De Layna